SIKH SOLDIER

Volume Seven

The Officer Corps

NARINDAR SINGH DHESI

Sikh Soldier

Volume Seven

The Officer Corps

An image of a Sikh Soldier in the stained glass window at Sandhurst

Dedication

To Laurie Michael Singh Dhesi,

I would like to express my profound respect and admiration to all Sikh officers that attendant:

Sandhurst

Woolwich

Cranwell

Dartmouth

Published by

The Naval & Military Press Ltd
Unit 5 Riverside, Brambleside
Bellbrook Industrial Estate
Uckfield, East Sussex
TN22 1QQ England

Tel: +44 (0) 1825 749494

www.naval-military-press.com
www.nmarchive.com

© Copyright Narinda Singh Dhesi

Contents

Dedication	3
Contents	5
Acknowledgements	6
Foreword	7
Sikh Soldier	9
Indian Army	14
Sandhurst	19
Malaysia	107
Sandurst (Malaysia)	108
Indian Artillery	121
Indian Engineers	125
Woolwich	127
Indian Air Force	136
Cranwell	143
Kenya	161
Royal Air Force	164
Indian Navy	177
British Armed Forces	212
Appendix	222
Bibliography	235
Index	237

Acknowledgements

Many people have given me enormous help in gathering the necessary information and material to write this account of the Sikh cadets that attended the famous 'Sandhurst', 'Woolwich', 'Cranwell', and 'Dartmouth' Academies in and their subsequent careers. Some of them have been gracious enough in allowing me to use their family's archive material, for which I am very grateful.

The curator at Sandhurst, Dr. Anthony Morton, has been kind in providing me with the list of the Indian cadets that attended Sandhurst. I have gleaned the names of the Sikh cadets from the list, and if I have missed any names, the blame lies entirely with me.

Thanks to Lieutenant General B.S. Dhaliwal (Retd) and Major General A.J.S. Sandhu (Retd) Indian Army, to provide me with the bio data of numerous Sikh officers without which this book would not have been written.

Thanks again to Lieutenant General B.S. Dhaliwal (Retd) for writing the Foreword for this book and also kindly scrutinizing my material.

Thanks to Vice Admiral Harinder Singh (Retd.), Indian Navy. He was persistent in gathering and providing me with the history of the Sikh Naval cadets that trained in Dartmouth, UK. He also wrote an article about of the Indian Navy.

Sincere thanks to Colonel Baldev Singh Johl (Retd), for his unstinting efforts in providing me with the bio data of the Malaysian Sikh officers.

Once again thanks to Major General A.J.S. Sandhu (Retd) for his kind comments about the book.

Foreword

During the First World War from 1914 to 1919, sixty thousand Indian soldiers had fought and died in blood-soaked battlefields from Europe to East Africa. The scale of their contribution can be judged from the fact that the Indian army earned no less than 9,200 decorations including 11 Victoria Crosses. Indeed, by November 1918 India had despatched 1,302,394 men to France; Mesopotamia; Egypt and Palestine; and smaller contingents to Aden, East Africa, Gallipoli, and Salonika. By contrast, all of the dominions together could only send 978,439 men. A thankful British government recognized this sacrifice.

In 1926, a Committee headed by Lieutenant General Andrew Skeen had noted that since 1918, eighty-five vacancies at Sandhurst were reserved exclusively for Indians. This would be followed by an increase of four per year until 1933, at which point an "Indian Sandhurst" with a capacity for 100 cadets would be established at Dehradun, as Sandhurst itself could not accommodate greater numbers.

Consequently, in the first half of the twentieth century the colonial Indian Army underwent a dramatic transition during which it was transformed into a relatively modern Army, complete with its own institutionalized Officer Corps. This impressive achievement was the culmination of a complex, if cautious, programme of social, political, and military reforms. Although these changes dramatically altered the character of the Army, and perhaps even the Nation, they practically have been ignored by the historiography on the Indian Army.

Foreword

Even the scant work done so far tends to underplay this crucial development. More importantly, the pioneer Officers who paved the way for the professionalization of the Indian Army has been largely ignored. This book by Narindar Singh Dhesi places on record the details of the Sikh Officers who contributed so largely to the development of a professional Officer Corps for their respective Armies. Narindar Singh Dhesi, with his enviable reputation for diligence, has painstakingly researched the details of the Sikh cadets who underwent training in England and traced their careers in the service of their Nations. From details of their social background, education and professional development, he has weaved a balanced and engrossing account of their biographies. It is a befitting continuation of his earlier books on Sikh Military History.

Dhaliwal B.S.
Lieutenant General (Retd)

Chandigarh

Lieutenant General (Retd) B.S. Dhaliwal, PVSM, AVSM, VSM, is a decorated soldier with a distinguished and chequered career, spanning 41 years, in the Corps of the Engineers of the Indian Army. Throughout his service, he has utilized his engineering knowledge and skills, with a capability and capacity to endure and to accomplish tasks, in a time-bound manner, during peace and war and in all terrain.

Sikh Soldier

India has a rich military tradition dating back to thousands of years with a definite science of warfare. There have been wars and campaigns involving men and Generals with exceptional capabilities. However, India was eventually overrun by the Muslim horde from central Asia, who set up their rule in India. At the time that Muslims (Mughals) established their rule in India, the people of the Punjab, who had borne the brunt of all the previous invasions, were sharply divided into separate religious societies. One, the Muslim, was an occupational army with their own kinsman as Subedars and Mansabdars and constantly sustained by fresh influx of Turkic and Afghan tribes, which practised fanaticism and intolerance. The other, the Hindu, rooted in idol worship, meaningless rituals and the degradation of caste system.

Meantime a remarkable people had emerged in the Punjab. They believed in the faith of Guru Nanak (Guru means a spiritual teacher and a guide). The chief doctrines preached by Guru Nanak were 'The Unity of God, Brotherhood of Man, Rejection of Caste and the futility of Idol Worship'. His followers became known as Sikhs.

The next hundred years from Guru Nanak's time saw the growth of a political movement alongside the religious movement, culminating in the call to arms by the last Sikh guru, Guru Gobind Singh. Within a few years after the death of Guru Gobind Singh, the Sikh peasants made the first attempt to liberate the Punjab from Mughal rule.

Sikh Soldier

Under the leadership of Banda Bahadur the Sikhs defied the authority of Mughal governors and kept the imperial armies at bay for a full seven years. Although Banda and his followers were ruthlessly slaughtered, the spark of the rebellion that they had lighted smouldered beneath the ashes and burst into flame again and again in different parts of the province.

"The Sikhs, it was thought had been hammered out of existence. But the hammering did not reduce them to pulp, but hardened the remnants to tempered steel." (V. Smith).

Under the guidance of Nawab Kapur Singh, a leading Sikh Sardar (chieftain), the Sikh Jathas (bands) were reorganized into twelve fighting units (misls). These Misls (meaning equals) operated independently of each other in the areas under their control, but facing common danger, merged under the banner of the Dal Khalsa (Sikh Army). As the hammer blows of Afghan invasions weakened the Mughal power, the Khalsa misls spread across the plains. Their enthusiasm was such that, against overwhelming odds, they overran most of central Punjab.

Eventually the Misl leaders, known as 'The Barons of the Horse', started carving out independent sovereign states in the Punjab.

The Sikh Confederacy (Dal Khalsa) evolved from a collection of small-to-medium sized independent sovereign Sikh states. They were loosely politically linked but strongly bound in cultural and religious spheres. As the Dal Khalsa grew, new regions were conquered and new Sikh Barons came to the fore.

Sikh Soldier

An ambitious young 'Baron of the Horse', Ranjit Singh of the Sukkarchakkia Confederacy, had inherited a force of 15,000 Horse and 5,000 Foot, with 6 pieces of artillery. He could also call on five feudal chiefs to supply him fighting contingents. From these humble beginnings, and by welding together the rude Barons of the Sikh Confederacy, he forged a powerful military machine that would not only overpower the outmoded and feudal armies of the petty principalities, but also contain the British, who were relentlessly expanding their frontiers. Maharajah Ranjit Singh single-mindedly modernized the Khalsa forces on European lines. He created and consolidated the most awesome military muscle ever seen in India, and became King of an Empire extending from Tibet to the deserts of Sindh, and from the Khyber Pass to the Satluj. His army was one of the most powerful at the time in all Asia. It was the first Indian force in a thousand years to carry invasion into the homelands of the traditional conquerors of India - the Pathans and the Afghans.

At the death of Maharajah Ranjit Singh, in the ensuing bloodletting between various competing factions for power, many a valiant Sardar had lost his life, and the survivors had bribed and used the Sikh Army for their own needs. Having no confidence in the ruling family and the executive, the Sikh Army (Khalsa) assumed control. The Khalsa vigorously resisted any foreign intervention in the State and proceeded to punish the traitors. The Sovereign and the leading Sardars frantically sought British intervention to save themselves.

Sikh Soldier

With the turmoil in the Punjab, and their underestimation of the fighting qualities of the Sikh soldier, the British started massing their armies; the largest force ever assembled in India, on the Kingdom's borders. The British also had an understanding of co-operation with Punjab Government Minister Gulab Singh Dogra, Chief Minister Lal Singh and the Commander-in-Chief Tej Singh, whose intention was to shatter the Khalsa on the British bayonets. As the British advanced on the Punjab, the Khalsa prepared for war.

"A powerful, well-trained, and confident Sikh army prepared for war under the leadership of a Commander-in-Chief under orders from a Vizier, and watched from the sidelines by a powerful and clever chieftain. All three men dedicated to the defeat of the army they lead, and secretly informing their British opponents of that fact!"
(Donald Featherstone)

Traitors on the field and traitors at court commanded the Khalsa armies; their main aim was the destruction of the Khalsa. Thus with ignominious treachery and deceit were sold the lives of the valiant soldiers of the Khalsa by their rulers, and thus was fought the First Anglo-Sikh War. At the conclusion of the war and the British victory the British government became the guardian of the young Maharajah Dalip Singh, and the Punjab became a British protectorate.

The district of Multan was a tributary of the Sikh Kingdom, and the revolt of the Hindu governor of Multan provided the excuse for the British annexation of the Punjab.

Sikh Soldier

As the remnants of the Khalsa rallied around the city of Multan, the British declared war on the Sikh Nation! The British invading forces deployed at various points in the Punjab were a staggering total of 104,666 men, comprising of 61,366 Regular British Army, 5,300 Lahore Army, 38,000 Irregular troops, plus 13,542 Cavalry, 123 Field guns and 22 Heavy guns.

At the conclusion of the First Anglo-Sikh War, the British had methodically destroyed the military power of the Sikhs. The soldiers had been disarmed, disbanded and dispersed. The pride of the Khalsa, the guns, were dismantled and taken away. What remained was but a shadow of the colossal military machine of Maharajah Ranjit Singh.

The major battle of the Second Sikh War was fought near Chillianwala. The British casualties amounted to 2,446 men, with 132 officers killed and 4 guns lost. Chillianwala was the worst defeat the British had suffered in their annals of Indian warfare. However, reinforced with fresh forces, they turned defeat into victory at the battle of Gujarat. The Punjab was annexed to British India, the Sikh Kingdom ended, and Maharajah Dalip Singh was pensioned off to England.

The Sikhs were considered the finest soldiers in the East. "If I had anything to say to annexation," Lord Harding had commented "I should enlist whole Regiments of Sikhs into our service."

The Sikhs were trained soldiers and knew no other calling and, when the offer came, flocked to the British standards.

Indian Army

However, some of the Sardars and Generals who had commanded the Khalsa armies served as Subedars in the British Indian Army. The Subedar's authority was confined to other Indian troops and he could not command British troops. Subedars became quite powerful and influential and were known as Viceroy's Commissioned Officers.

The Indian Army had been proud of possessing a triple function; the preservation of internal peace in India itself, the defence of Indian Frontiers; and preparedness to embark at a moment's notice in other parts of the world. In this third aspect Indian Army provided the British Government with a striking force always ready, of admirable efficiency, and assured valour. They not only extended, but secured and sustained the British Empire.

During the First World War a large number of Indian troops was dispatched to various battle fields in support of British armies and suffered very heavy casualties, and scripted many victories with their valour and sacrifice in numerous battlefields.

That the Indian Expeditionary Force arrived in France and Flanders in the nick of time, and helped to save the cause both of the Allies and of civilization, after the sanguinary tumult of the opening weeks of the War, has been acknowledged by the highest in the land, from the Sovereign downwards. It would be truer to say that the Indian Corps saved the Empire. (Merewether and Fredrick Smith Bart)

Indian Army

Their deeds of valour and sacrifice brought much credit to the Indian arms, and they clamoured for Indian officer corps to be established. Britain had after all to bow down to their demands and send the cadets to be commissioned as officers at the Royal Military Academy Sandhurst. On completion of training, they were to be granted the coveted King's Commission in the Indian Army. An option for training at Royal Military College, Woolwich, for entry into arms other than infantry and cavalry continued, as did the training at Cranwell for the airmen and Dartmouth for the sailors. There was great disquiet amongst the British, who disliked the idea of serving under native officers; others felt that without good breeding, a public school education, and sufficient suitable training, Indians would not become good officers and would neither be able to lead nor be accepted by the native troops.

There was a firm belief among British officers and the home government that only the British educational system could provide the right kind of officer, and that it could do it only from suitable stock. Sandhurst, Woolwich, Cranwell and Dartmouth, training directly pitted young Indian men against young Europeans in conditions alien to their upbringing and experience and in spite of obstructions by the British, proved their gallantry and leadership during the Second World War.

In August 1947, at the time of the independence and division of the subcontinent into sovereign states of India and Pakistan, the subcontinent was plunged in a great turmoil due to widespread communal riots.

Indian Army

The movement of Muslims and non-Muslims (Sikhs and Hindus) were matched evenly in Punjab. Both sides perpetrated the worst type of savagery. The entire population of the region appeared to have gone berserk. The situation created major administrative problems and the Indian Army had to step in to control the situation. The Sikh officers were called into man the higher ranks of the Indian Army to control the situation.

Immediately after independence, tensions between India and Pakistan began to boil over, and the first of three full-scale wars between the two nations broke out over the then princely state of Kashmir. The Maharaja of Kashmir wanted to maintain the status quo. Since Kashmir was a Muslim majority state, Pakistan wanted to make Kashmir a Pakistan territory. In 1948 Pakistan invaded Kashmir and, as a result, Maharaja Hari Singh appealed to India for help. He signed the Instrument of Accession to India. It took two weeks for Indian forces to reach the war front. Pakistan suffered significant losses. Most neutral assessments agree that India was the victor of the war as it was able to conquer about two-thirds of Kashmir, including Kashmir valley, Jammu and Ladakh.

After the partition of India, the State of Hyderabad, a princely state under the rule of a Nizam, chose to remain independent. The Nizam refused to cede his state to the Union of India. The following stand-off between the Government of India and the Nizam ended on 12TH September 1948 when India's then deputy Prime Minister Sardar Vallabhbhai Patel ordered Indian troops to secure the state.

Indian Army

With five days of low-intensity fighting, the Indian Army, backed by a squadron of Hawker Tempest aircraft of the Indian Air Force, routed the Hyderabad State forces. Five infantry Battalions and one armoured squadron of the Indian Army were engaged in the operation. The following day, the State of Hyderabad was proclaimed as a part of the Union of India.

Portugal refused to relinquish control of its Indian colonies of Goa, Daman and Diu. After repeated attempts by India to negotiate with Portugal for the territory were spurned by the Portuguese prime minister and dictator, India launched Operation Vijay on 12TH December 1961 to take Goa from the Portuguese. A small contingent of its troops entered Goa, Daman, and Diu to capture and secure the territory. After a brief conflict, the Portuguese surrendered to the Indian Army, and Goa, Daman and Diu joined the Indian Union.

Small-scale clashes between the Indian and Chinese forces broke out as India insisted on the disputed McMahon Line being regarded as the international border between the two countries. After a series of failed negotiations, the People's Liberation Army attacked Indian Army positions at the Thag La ridge. This move by China caught India by surprise and by 12TH October, Nehru gave orders for the Chinese to be expelled from Aksai Chin. However, poor coordination among various Divisions of the Indian Army and the late decision to mobilise the Indian Air Force in vast numbers gave China a crucial tactical and strategic advantage over India.

Indian Army

On 20TH October, Chinese soldiers attacked India in both the North-West and North-Eastern parts of the border and captured vast portions of Aksai Chin and Arunachal Pradesh.

The Sino-Indian conflict of 1962 lasted for just two months. The Indians' 'brink of the war' doctrine, the brain child of Lieutenant General B.M. Kaul, supposed to regain the lost Aksai Chin, went out of control, exploded and fell and resulted in the unnecessary war. The Indian Army was not prepared for it, but still gave a tough fight and made the Chinese Army halt their advance at just the foothills, declare a unilateral cease fire and retrace its steps.

This is the narrative of the Sikh cadets of India, Kenya, Malaysia and United Kingdom that graduated from Sandhurst, Woolwich, Cranwell, and Dartmouth, the crucial role they played, and currently are playing, in the defence of their respective countries with an unflinching sense of duty, discipline and traditions of valour of the Sikhs.

Narindar Singh Dhesi

Sandhurst

The Royal Military Academy Sandhurst (RMAS), commonly known simply as Sandhurst, is the British Army's initial officer training centre and is located in the town of Camberley, near the village of Sandhurst, Berkshire, about 55 kilometres (34 mi) southwest of London. The Academy's stated aim is to be "the national centre of excellence for leadership". All British Army officers, including late-entry officers who were previously Warrant Officers, as well as other men and women from overseas, are trained at Sandhurst.

Sandhurst

Prince Victor Duleep Singh
Commissioned from the RMAS in 1887
At the age of eleven, Maharajah Duleep Singh, ruler of the Sikh Kingdom, was removed from his kingdom by the British after the Anglo-Sikh Wars and exiled to Britain. There he combined the extraordinary lifestyle of an Indian Prince, redesigning his Suffolk residence, Eleveden Hall, in the style of a Mughal palace, with the gentrification of a young aristocrat, associating with the cream of Victorian Society.

As a young man Prince Victor Duleep Singh studied at Eton before going up to Cambridge, where he met his first true love, Lady Ann Blanche Alice of Coventry.

He was the first known person of Sikh descent (for that matter, a man of colour) who entered the Royal Military College, Sandhurst in 1887, with a special Cadetship. Children of Indian extraction were disqualified by parentage from the Army under the existing rules, but Queen Victoria bent the rules for her godson. The Prince graduated from Sandhurst the following December to be commissioned as 2ND Lieutenant into the 1ST (Royal) Dragoons. He was promoted to Captain in 1894. In 1889 he was stationed at Halifax, Nova Scotia, as a member of the staff of General Sir John Ross, commander of British forces in British North America. He continued serve in the Royal Dragoons until he resigned his commission in 1898. On the death of his father on 23RD October 1893, Prince Victor succeeded him as Head of the Royal House of the Punjab.

Sandhurst

Prince Victor Duleep Singh
On 4TH January 1898, Prince Victor Duleep Singh married Lady Anne Coventry, a daughter of George William Coventry, 9TH Earl of Coventry, and the marriage created a sensation. It was the first time an Indian Prince had married an English Noblewoman. The wedding took place at St Peter's Church, Eaton Square, London.

Soon after the wedding, Princess Victor, Anne's title after the marriage, was asked for a private audience with Her Majesty. The queen told Anne that she must never have any children with Prince Victor. Princess Victor complied with her sovereign's wishes. There would never be another Duleep Singh's heir to challenge for the throne of the Punjab!

Prince Victor Duleep Singh died, without legitimate issue, aged 51, on 7TH June 1918, and was buried at the Anglican Cemetery above Monte Carlo.

Prince Frederick Duleep Singh
Commissioned in the British Army in 1893
Prince Frederick Duleep Singh was born on 23RD January 1868 at Rutland Gate, Knightsbridge. He completed his education by first going to Eton College, Berkshire, and then to Magdalene College, Cambridge, where in 1890 he gained a master's degree in history.

He enrolled in the Loyal Suffolk Hussars (Suffolk Yeomanry) in the Regiment's centenary year, and was appointed Second Lieutenant on 12TH August 1893.

Sandhurst

Prince Frederick Duleep Singh
He was promoted to Captain in 1898 and was admitted a Member of the Royal Victorian Order in 1901, which was designed for recognition of personal services to Queen Victoria. In the same year he transferred to the King's Own Royal Regiment Norfolk Imperial Yeomanry and was promoted to the rank of Major.

The Prince resigned his commission in 1908, but rejoined as a Major in October 1914 on the outbreak of the First World War. He was gazetted to the 2ND Battalion, 1ST Norfolk Yeomanry, serving in France from 1917 to 1918. He spent much time with training units, and was at a rest camp for artillery horses, where he was area commandant.

In 1926, Prince Frederick Duleep Singh fell critically ill. During the previous few months his health had been in decline, but on Thursday 12TH August 1926, he suffered a heart attack. His sisters immediately surrounded him and the family received a message of inquiry from the King on the Saturday. Sadly, the much loved last Prince of Lahore passed away at Blo Norton Hall at 2.30 p.m. on Sunday afternoon, 15TH August, at the age of fifty eight, The funeral took place the following Thursday at St. Andrew's Church in Blo Norton, Suffolk.

The wheeled bier was met by the chief mourners, Princesses Bamba, Catherine and Sophie. Among those attending were a great many local folk, including representatives and friends of the various societies and organisations with which Prince Frederick was associated, with many other landed gentry and officials.

Sandhurst

Prince Frederick Duleep Singh
The Prince was the last male heir of the illustrious Sikh Durbar. Tragically, to keep peace with the authorities, Prince Frederick never set foot in the Punjab to witness the marvels over which his family's rule had extended. His death put an end to the legacy of the Sikh Kingdom.

Colonel Daya Singh Bedi
Commissioned from the RMAS in 1921
Sardar Daya Singh Bedi was born in 1899 to Raja Sir Gurbaksh Singh Bedi K.B.E., Kt., and C.L.E. He was the direct descendant of Sri Guru Nanak. Daya Singh Bedi graduated from the Sandhurst Academy on 14TH July 1921, was commissioned as a Second Lieutenant and rose to the rank of Lieutenant before being transferred in September 1928 to the Indian Political Service. He was subsequently given the honorary rank of Lieutenant Colonel during his military assignment in Nepal.

He achieved promotions from 1928 till 1937 as Political Agent (1931, Southern States and Central India), Undersecretary (1932, States of Western India), Assistant Commissioner in the Princely states of Rajputana (1933), Travancore (1935) and Orissa Province (1937). Bedi also had responsibilities inherited with his title in Pashtunistan and the Punjab region. He served with distinction as an officer of the Indian Civil Service (British India) in the regions where his family patronage existed and had a record of reconstruction and administrative efficiency in the aftermath of the earthquake.

Sandhurst

Colonel Daya Singh Bedi

Bedi was the Political Resident in Quetta-Pishin District till 1938, Political Resident of Loralai, Baluchistan, Pakistan from 1939 to 1941, Political Resident and Deputy Commissioner of Hazara, North-West Frontier Province from 1942 to 1944, Political Agent Kurram in 1945, Political Agent Orissa States from 1946-47, Regional Commissioner Rajputana in 1948.

At Indian independence, Bedi joined the newly formed Ministry of External Affairs and Commonwealth Relations which was later renamed Ministry of External Affairs (India) in the Indian Foreign Service department. His negotiation was instrumental in the amicable Division of weapons, equipment, Regiments and rights of the Gurkhas in military service of India and was a signatory to the Britain-India-Nepal Tripartite Agreement. The following year in 1948 he was appointed as the Indian High Commissioner to Australia and served till 1951. On his return to India, Bedi was appointed as Chief Commissioner of Coorg State where he served till 1956 when the province was dissolved and merged with the neighbouring Mysore State. On retirement, Baba Daya Singh Bedi studied Sufi poetry. Colonel Daya Singh Bedi passed away in 1975.

Sandhurst

Brigadier Gurbachan Singh
Commissioned from the RMAS in 1923

Sardar Gurbachan was the son of Sardar Gopal Singh of Bhagowal. He was born in 1905 and was educated at Khalsa College Amritsar. Sardar Gopal Singh was a direct commissioned officer to the rank of Jemadar in the 11TH Prince of Wales' Own Bengal Lancers, later known as 11TH Prince of Wales' Lancers and eventually from July 1904 redesignated as Probyn's Horse. At the time of his joining the Regiment in 1889, The Colonel-in-Chief was the King, and one of his Regimental officer's was Lt. Col. Birdwood, who went on to become the Commander-in-Chief of The British Indian Army.

This was the connection that sent Sardar Gurbachan Singh to the Royal Military College at Sandhurst for training in 1923. As a 2ND Lieutenant he did his attachment with a British Cavalry Regiment the 4TH Hussars and on completion of the attachment was posted to 7TH Light Cavalry, one of the three Indian Regiments, located at Sialkot. He served for the maximum time in Alpha Squadron comprising of Jats. In the Regiment he was rechristened 'Baby Gurbachan' on account of a youthful face with a very little beard. He was an accomplished horseman and polo player and served as the Regimental polo secretary for almost a decade, during which period he played a pivotal role in winning a series of Polo tournaments for the Regiment, including the prestigious Hyderabad Open Polo Championship in November 1937. He was also a good shot and keen huntsman, both qualities inherited from his father.

Sandhurst

Brigadier Gurbachan Singh

During the early years of his career, Gurbachan Singh moved twice with the Regiment, first to the Central Indian state of Hyderabad and later to Loralai in Baluchistan. Interestingly the Regiments use to move on horseback with Junior Commissioned Officers responsible for the men. The officers accompanying the Regiment were allowed to hunt and shoot en route.

Life carried on at a leisurely pace till Hitler's Germany overran Poland and Czechoslovakia. The Indian army was also mobilized for war, the majority of the forces going to Egypt. When the Japanese threat erupted in the East, as they overran Malaya and threatened Burma and Assam, Seventh Light Cavalry was earmarked for conversion to Stuart Light Tank as part of the 254 Tank Brigade for Burma. But all Indian officers of the rank Captain and above were posted out of the Regiment. Captain Gurbachan Singh and Major T.S. Bal were posted out to Recruit Training Centre in Lucknow. Captain Gurbachan Singh later opted for the Remount and Veterinary Corps (RVC) and was posted to Sargodha depot in West Punjab, where he remained till the partition of India in 1947. Amidst the tumult and violence of Partition, a Baluch escort delivered him safely to the newly created Wagah Border on the Grand Trunk Road with Pakistan.

Thereafter he was posted as Director Remount and Vetenary Services at the Army Headquarters in Simla in the rank of Brigadier.

Sandhurst

Brigadier Gurbachan Singh

He was there to witness history in the making with the departure of Lord Mountbatten as the last Viceroy of India and the nomination of C. Gopalcahri as the Governor General of India. Subsequently he was posted as Sub-Area Commander in Madras and had the interesting opportunity to live in the same palatial house as Lord Robert Clive in Fort Saint George. He then attended the senior officers' Staff College at Wellington in Connor and thereafter at his own request was posted to North India as Sub Area Commander Meerut.

In 1951 he took premature retirement when he did not make it to the rank of Major General. His decision not to serve under a junior officer, as well as the passing away of his father at the time, led him to leave the army to look after the family landholdings and settle down in Gurdaspur in Punjab. He is survived by three sons; the oldest Sardar Amarjit Singh served in the tea gardens of Assam. His second son, Lieutenant Colonel Paramjit Singh retired from the Territorial Army. The youngest joined the very same Seventh Light Cavalry and rose to retire as a Lieutenant General in the Indian Army. And his son, Colonel Vikramjit Singh Kahlon now continues the family tradition, following in his father's and grandfather's footsteps and has recently commanded the 7TH Light Cavalry.

(Info supplied by Colonel Vikramjit Singh Kahlon via Major General A.J.S. Sandhu).

Sandhurst

Captain Balwant Singh Lamba
Commissioned from the RMAS in 1924

Sardar Balwant Singh Lamba was born in 1903, into the illustrious Sikh family of Sardar Tara Singh. Sardar Balwant Singh Lamba was first cousin of Sardar Swarn Singh Lamba of Pindilala, descendant of General Sardar Gurmukh Singh Lamba, an eminent general of Maharajah Ranjit Singh, the sovereign of the Sikh Kingdom. Sardar Tara Singh was wounded fifteen times and he was the recipient of the highest military award the Izat-e-Sardari, and civil awards of Nirmal Bud, Uja Didar. His portrait sketch painting is displayed at Central Museum Lahore, Pakistan.

Balwant Singh later moved to Baradari, where he completed his education, joined the Indian Army and was sent to the Military Academy, Sandhurst in UK, for further training. After receiving his commission from officer training at Sandhurst on 27TH August 1924, he permanently joined the 4TH Battalion, 19TH Hyderabad Regiment, and served in Iraq, Allahabad, Fort Sandeman, and Quetta 1927-36.

During the Second World War, he served in Malaya 1939-40; he proceeded to Burma with 25TH Indian Infantry Division, and served there until the Japanese surrender in 1945. At the time of the partition of the subcontinent, into India and Pakistan in 1947, he lost the family land in West Pakistan, and decided to leave the Army with the rank of Captain. In the early years he managed the vast property and affairs of his mother in law, who was a widow, at Bashirpur Pur.

Sandhurst

Captain Balwant Singh Lamba
Eventually in exchange of the lands lost to him in West Pakistan, he was allotted a large holding at Mushsir, Ferozepore district (His and his wife's share and the wife's elder sister as she was not married and stayed with them after partition). Sardar Balwant Singh Lamba passed away at Mushirm, due to a massive heart attack. His son Mahabir Singh Lamba, who retired as a Major from the Army, was murdered while looking after his landed property. As there were no heirs to inherit the vast estate, it was appropriated by the state.

(Info supplied by Colonel Harjeet Singh Lamba)

Major General Gurdip Singh Dhillon
Commissioned from the RMAS in 1924
Sardar Gurdip Singh Dhillon graduated from the Sandhurst Military Academy and was commissioned 27TH August 1924. After serving a year in a British Regiment, he was posted to 1ST Battalion, 14TH Punjab Regiment. Initially he served in the same Regiment on the North-West Frontier Province. Much happened in the years spent on the Frontier and by this time Gurdip Singh Dhillon had attained the rank of Captain, and had been appointed as the Adjutant of the Regiment. The Regiment had scarcely settled down at Jhelum when the Mohmad operations intervened. In 1933 dissentions between the Upper and Lower Mohmands over the latter's loyalty to Government led to the former, under the Haji of Turangzai, invading the Gandar Valley.

Sandhurst

Major General Gurdip Singh Dhillon

The Regiment had to intervene and the Gandar Valley MT Road had been built to just short of the Nahakki Pass. Failure to insist on its extension over that historic high ground was interpreted by the Upper Mohmands as weakness, and led them to truculence. They refused to hand over certain outlaws; they quarrelled with the Lower Mohmands over the distribution of the road contract money; and finally in mid-August they started to demolish the road. Their Lashkar at first numbered 1,400 Burhan Khel and Isa Khel, but soon greatly increased from the Safis and other tribes.

Advancing on 23RD August, two brigades, including the Regiment, reached Ghalanai next day against appreciable opposition and during the next few days cleared the locality and established the Line of Control. Before extending the road over the Nahakki Pass, it was decided to increase the force. All officers and men on leave in India were recalled, and the depot under Lieutenant Vir Singh was left behind in Jhelum. The first operation of significance was the passage of the Nahakki Pass. The Battalion left Ghalanai and spent time building the road over to Nahakki, while the enemy harassed all they could. On the 14TH September, the Battalion laid a successful ambush for the enemy parties now actively sniping Wucha Jawar Camp. The sniping could be plainly heard over the ridge and soon became very heavy. Some fourteen of the snipers bumped into No.4 Platoon, which opened fire at twenty yards.

Sandhurst

Major General Gurdip Singh Dhillon
While some fell, the remainder of the enemy ran left, until ambushed at very close range by No. 2 Platoon and suffered further casualties. Five minutes later much the same was repeated by another batch of tribesmen. Both parties now moved further west until they were shot of the muzzles of Nos. 1 and 5 Platoons. This virtually ended the operation. The tribes submitted on 3RD October.

In 1937 Captain Gurdip Singh Dhillon was transferred to the RIASC. While still on the Frontier he took part in the Bahadur Khel operations in 1938. He also saw action in the operations around Ahmedzai Salient near Bannu during 1939-1940.

From the Frontier he proceeded to the Middle East 1941. The Middle East Theatre was a major theatre of operations during the Second World War. The vast size of the Middle East theatre saw interconnected naval, land, and air campaigns fought for control of North Africa, the Horn of Africa, the Middle East and Southern Europe. The fighting in this theatre lasted from 10TH June 1940, when Italy entered the war on the side of Nazi Germany, until all Axis forces in Italy surrendered.

At the rank of Major, Gurdip Singh Dhillon attended 6TH War Course Staff College at Quetta. He was then appointed Officer Commanding 7TH Motor Transport Regiment ALFSEA in 1944. He was posted to Imphal, Burma in 1945 and joined the 25TH Infantry Division. In 1946 he was appointed the Deputy Director (Petrol Oil and Lubrication) at the Army Headquarters.

Sandhurst

Major General Gurdip Singh Dhillon
On 24TH November 1947, at the time of Indian Independence, he was the first Indian Officer to be appointed Director Supply and Transport, and remained Director throughout Jammu and Kashmir Operations in 1947. In 1949 he was appointed General Officer Commanding Uttar Pradesh. The Command was for looking after the various administrative units located in the UP area. (Uttar Pradesh is incidentally one of the states of India). He retired from the Indian Army on grounds of ill health on 18TH August 1950.
Major General Gurdip Singh Dhillon passed away on the 14TH February 1952.

Major General Bakshish Singh Chimni OBE
Commissioned from the RMAS in 1924
Sardar Bakshish Singh Chimni was born on August 28TH 1905 in Gujranwala, Punjab. He studied in Khalsa High School and passed matriculation examination with Distinction and set a record which has not been broken. Later he joined the prestigious Government College Lahore where he was selected to undergo training at the Royal Military Academy Sandhurst, England. He graduated from the Academy and was commissioned as a 2ND Lieutenant in August 30TH. 1924. He was initially attached to the Royal Scots Fusiliers for a year and was then posted to the 5TH Royal Mahratta.

His father and elder brother had seen service in the First World War with the 12TH Sam Browne's Cavalry. Since he was from a Cavalry background, he asked to be posted to a Cavalry Regiment.

Sandhurst

Major General Bakshish Singh Chimni OBE
Since there was no vacancy in a Cavalry Regiment, he was transferred to the Royal Indian Army Service Corps. He took part in the Mohmand operations in the Northern Western frontier of India against the turbulent tribesman. He got a competitive vacancy in entrance exam to the Staff College Quetta, and attended the 1938 course, achieving a distinction. He served in Burma with the 7TH Indian Division during the Second World War, as the Assistant Adjutant and Quartermaster General in Headquarters 101 Line of Control Area. In recognition of his meritorious services, he was Mentioned in Dispatches twice and later bestowed with the OBE (i.e. Officer of the Order of the British Empire on 1ST January 1945).

In 1947 when the Partition of the Country was decided upon, he was selected to be a member of the Partition Committee of the Army. He played an important role in dividing the Army's assets. Units with predominantly Muslim composition went to Pakistan and the Weaponry and the Equipment etc was proportionately divided between India and Pakistan. When the communal riots started in 1947, and the Hindu and Sikhs were to be evacuated from areas which went to Pakistan and Muslims to Pakistan, a Military evacuation organization (MEO) was setup and Prime Minister Nehru personally selected him as the Commanding Officer of this organization. At this juncture only three officers were promoted to the rank of Major General, namely K.M. Carriappa, Rajindra Sinhji, and Sardar Bakshish Singh Chimni.

Sandhurst

Major General Bakshish Singh Chimni OBE
Major General Bakshish Singh Chimni was appointed as a Commander of the Military evacuation. It is pertinent to mention that Utter Chaos prevailed in the Country at that time. General Chimni setup his HQ in Amritsar. There were no troops or transport and any other infrastructure that was provided. He commandeered the offices, units and transport passing through Amritsar on return from Pakistan and attached them under his command and commenced his operations of Refugee Camp without any allotment of troops or transport from the Government. With all these constraints, and no logistical support, General Chimni evacuated 7 Lacks Refugees in one month.

At this juncture because of his aggressive attitude and the method of operating, the Government in their wisdom choose to transfer him, despite many strong protests from the Punjabis. The newspapers and editorials protested, and wanted an explanation with regards to Major General Chimni's transfer. The Government came out with an explanation that he had been transferred as he had been earmarked for higher appointments. Then Major General Chimni was posted to Eastern Command located in Ranchi (Bihar) as (MGA) as Major General in charge administration. From Ranchi he was posted to Army HQ where he held twin appointments of the Quartermaster General and Master General Ordinance. From Army HQ's he was posted as General Officer Commanding Uttar Pradesh area from where he retired in 1955.

Sandhurst

Major General Bakshish Singh Chimni OBE
He moved to his farm in Tarai area in the foothills of Nanital. General Chimni passed away on 14TH December 1977 in Lucknow. It would be pertinent to mention that 7 generations of the Chimni family served in the Army including his four sons. During 1965 Indo-Pak War all four sons saw active service the Battle. General Chimni's ancestors, General Hukma Singh Chimni and General Hari Singh Nalwa served together in Maharaja Ranjit Singh Army.
(Info supplied by the General's son, Colonel Birindar Singh Chimni).

Lieutenant General Sant Singh
Commissioned from the RMAS in 1925
Sardar Sant Singh was born on November $28^{TH.}$ 1903, at Dakha village in the vicinity of Mullanpur in Ludhiana district in the Indian state of Punjab, to Dafadar Sewa Singh and Sardarni Kishan Kaur. He got his primary education at his village and then got admission in Arya High School Ludhiana from where he matriculated. Then he got admission in 1921 in Khalsa College Amritsar for higher studies. In 1923 he was recommended by the principal of the college for commission in the army. Consequently he was sent to Sandhurst Military Academy in UK. He graduated from Sandhurst and was commissioned on 29TH January 1925, with the rank of 2ND Lieutenant. After serving a year in a British Regiment, he was posted to 1ST Battalion, 14TH Punjab on the North-West Frontier Province of India.

Sandhurst

Lieutenant General Sant Singh

Much happened in the years spent on the Frontier; the comings and goings on courses and leaves; the annual and General's inspections; success in sports and games; competitions for Regimental and Indian Army shooting trophies; visitors; epidemics; the road protection duties and hill training was undertaken.

By this time Sant Singh had attained the rank of Captain. The Regiment had scarcely settled down at Jhelum when the Mohmad operations intervened. In 1933 dissentions between the Upper and Lower Mohmands over the latter's loyalty to Government led to the former under the Haji of Turangzai invading the Gandar Valley. The Regiment had to intervene and the Gandar Valley MT Road had been built to just short of the Nahakki Pass. Failure to insist on its extension over that historic high ground was interpreted by the Upper Mohmands as weakness, and led them to truculence. They refused to hand over certain outlaws; they quarrelled with the Lower Mohmands over the distribution of the road contract money; and finally in mid-August they started to demolish the road. Their Lashkar at first numbered 1,400 Burhan Khel and Isa Khel, but soon greatly increased from the Safis and other tribes. Advancing on 23RD August, two brigades, including the Regiment, reached Ghalanai next day against appreciable opposition and during the next few days cleared the locality and established the Line of Control. Before extending the road over the Nahakki Pass, it was decided to increase the force.

Sandhurst

Lieutenant General Sant Singh

All officers and men on leave in India were recalled, and the depot under Lieutenant Vir Singh was left behind in Jhelum. The first operation of significance was the passage of the Nahakki Pass. The Battalion left Ghalanai and spent time building the road over to Nahakki, while the enemy harassed all they could. On 14TH, the Battalion laid a successful ambush for the enemy parties now actively sniping Wucha Jawar Camp. The sniping could be plainly heard over the ridge, and soon became very heavy. Some fourteen of the snipers bumped into No. 4 Platoon, which opened fire at twenty yards. While some fell the remainder of the enemy ran left, until ambushed at very close range by No. 2 Platoon and suffered further casualties. Five minutes later much the same was repeated by another batch of tribesmen. Both parties now moved further west until they were shot of the muzzles of Nos. 1 and 5 Platoons. This virtually ended the operation. The tribes submitted on 3RD October. The Battalion went on to mount punitive expeditions in Waziristan in 1937-38. By taking part in the Waziristan operations the Battalion earned another clasp to the Indian General Service Medal.

On the eve of the Second World War, Major Sant Singh was transferred as Second-in-Command to the Bihar Regiment. The Bihar Regiment had been formed by the 11TH (Territorial) Battalion, 19TH Hyderabad Regiment in 1941. Major Sant Singh commanded the 2ND Battalion, Bihar Regiment and took part in the Operation Zipper, for the reconquest of Malaya.

Sandhurst

Lieutenant General Sant Singh

At the time of India's partition he was promoted Colonel, and headed one of the special selection Boards at Yol Camp. Due to the partition the army faced a shortage of officers and to meet this challenge, Emergency Commissioned Officers were recruited and they were put through a short course and then they were selected for permanent commission.

As Brigadier he commanded the 43RD Army Brigade and entrusted with the task of refugee caravans coming to India from Pakistan through Hussainiwala Border. As a Major General he took over the command of the famous 'Red Eagles', 4TH Infantry Division, as a nucleus of the Punjab Boundary Force. After this posting he was posted out to Army HQs as Master General of ordnance (M.C.O.). The logistics function of the Army Ordnance Corps involves the mechanics of provisioning and procuring of all stores required to raise and maintain an efficient and effective fighting army. The aim of Army Ordnance Corps is to make available all kinds of stores to all units of the army at the right time, in right quantity, at the right place and right cost. Further, the inventory range covers every conceivable requirement of the soldier from clothing to weapons, from a needle to a tank and also all munitions except fuel, fodder and medicines. The inventory management functions involve provisioning, procurement, receipt, accounting, storage, issue, transportation and disposal of all clothing, equipment, weapons, vehicles, ammunition and spares of all kinds.

Sandhurst

Lieutenant General Sant Singh
Ammunition management is another important function of Army Ordnance Corps. He remained there till 1951. In 1951 Sant Singh was promoted Lieutenant General and was appointed G.O.C. Eastern Command. The Eastern Command of the Indian Army is one of the seven operational commands of the army. The Command was later split into two commands i.e., Central Command and Eastern Command.

In May 1957, General S.M. Shrinagesh retired, and General Thimayya was nominated to succeed him as Chief of Army Staff, by the Prime Minister Nehru, superseding Lieutenant General Sant Singh, who was commanding the Eastern Army, and was senior to General Thimayya. He was the first Sikh officer to be bypassed and superseded. Consequently Lieutenant General Sant Singh put in his papers and retired from the Army in disgust. However during his tenure of service he was 'Mentioned in Despatches', and was also appointed Honorary ADC to the President of India.

He took keen interest in the development of sports. He was made Director of the National Institute of Sports at Patiala for three years. He also took keen interest in farming and development of agriculture. He was the President of the Kisan Club in Pau at Ludhiana, and devoted himself to the farming at his village Dakha. He carried on this with deep interest till his death on November $27^{TH,}$ 1975.

Sandhurst

Lieutenant General Kalwant Singh
Commissioned from the RMAS in 1925

Sardar Kalwant Singh was born at Rawalpindi (now Pakistan) on April $23^{RD,}$ 1905. He was educated at Rawalpindi and then sent to Royal Military Academy, Sandhurst, for officer training. He graduated from the Academy and was commissioned on January 29TH, 1925, with the rank of 2ND Lieutenant. Before joining his parent Regiment, the 2ND Battalion, 1ST Punjab Regiment, he served a year with a British Regiment.

2ND Lieutenant Kalwant Singh was one of the first Indian Officers to join the 2ND Battalion, 1ST Punjab Regiment in 1926. The 2ND Battalion spent practically the whole of the period between the two World Wars on the North-West Frontier. While serving on the Frontier, Kalwant Singh was involved in extensive fighting. The main actions were fought against: (The Mohmands 1927), (Red Shirt Rebellion 1930-31), (Bajour 1933), (Loe Agra Campaign), (Second Mohmand Campaign), and (Waziristan 1936-39).

In 1944, a British committee under Lieutenant-General Sir Francis Tucker was set up to review future policy for the region. As part of its findings, it recommended the withdrawal of all regular forces from tribal territory into outposts, or cantonments, along the administrative border from where they could keep an eye on things. The un-administered districts would then once again become the responsibility of the local militias, and the Regiment was withdrawn from the North-West Frontier Province.

Sandhurst

Lieutenant General Kalwant Singh

During the Second World War, with surprising rapidity, the Japanese had pushed back the Allied Forces in Burma to the Indian border. It was not only essential to stop the Japanese from invading India, but also imperative to regain Burma. The 2ND Battalion was mobilised in February, 1942 as a part of the 47TH Brigade and joined the 14TH Indian Division on April 5TH. In October, 1942, the 14TH Division mounted offensive operations against the Japanese in the first Arakan campaign and recaptured Donbaik and Hitzwe. At Buthidaung Major Sarbjit Singh Kalha took over the command of the Battalion. He was the first Indian to command a Battalion of the Regiment. Meanwhile, in November, 1943, now Lieutenant Colonel Kalwant Singh took over the command of the 7TH Battalion stationed at Razmak.

In September, 1944, the 7TH Battalion, prepared to move to the operational area in South-East Asia. However, the Japanese surrendered in August, 1945.

The Battalion was stationed in Singapore at the time of the Partition of India and the Sikhs formed part of the Army of the Republic of India.

At the conclusion of the First Anglo-Sikh War (1845–46) Gulab Singh became the first Maharaja of the newly formed princely state of Jammu and Kashmir. Before and after the withdrawal of the British from India in 1947; the princely state of Kashmir and Jammu came under pressure from both India and Pakistan to agree to become part of one of the newly independent countries.

Sandhurst

Lieutenant General Kalwant Singh

As the Maharaja of Kashmir, Hari Singh acceded to India; the Pakistani Army backed the tribal infiltrators that invaded the Kashmir Valley. Immediately the Indian troops were sent to the state to defend it. On 8TH September 1947, Jammu and Kashmir forces Headquarters was set up in Jammu under the command of now Major General Kalwant Singh. In April 1948 the forces in Jammu and Kashmir were re-organized and Major General Kalwant Singh was appointed Chief of Staff of the Corps. India airlifted troops and equipment to Srinagar, where they reinforced the princely state forces, established a defence perimeter and defeated the tribal forces on the outskirts of the city. The successful defence included an outflanking manoeuvre by Indian armoured cars. The defeated tribal forces were pursued as far as Baramula and Uri and these towns were recaptured.

In the Poonch valley, tribal forces continued to besiege state forces. Indian forces ceased pursuit of tribal forces after recapturing Uri and Baramula, and sent a relief column southwards, in an attempt to relieve Poonch. Although the relief column eventually reached Poonch, the siege could not be lifted.

After capturing Mirpur on 25TH of November 1947, the tribal forces attacked and captured Jhangar. In the south an Indian attack secured Chhamb. By this stage of the war the front line began to stabilize as more Indian troops became available. The Indians held onto Jhangar against numerous counterattacks, which were increasingly supported by regular Pakistani Forces.

Sandhurst

Lieutenant General Kalwant Singh
The Indians recaptured Tithwal and continued to attack, driving north to capture Keran and Gurais. They also repelled a counterattack aimed at Tithwal. `
The surprise attack on 1ST November by the Brigade with armour supported by two Regiments of 25 pounders and a Regiment of 3.7 inch guns, forced the pass and pushed the tribal/Pakistani forces back to Matayan and later Dras. The Brigade linked up on 24TH November at Kargil with Indian troops advancing from Leh, while their opponents eventually withdrew northwards toward Iskardu. The Indians now started to get the upper hand in all sectors. Poonch was finally relieved after a siege of over a year. The Indians pursued the Pakistanis as far as Kargil before being forced to halt due to supply problems. The Zojila La pass was forced by using tanks and Dras was recaptured.
At this stage the Indian Prime Minister, Jawaharlal Nehru, decided to ask the UN to intervene. A UN cease-fire was arranged for 31ST December 1948. A few days before the cease-fire the Pakistanis launched a counter attack, which cut the road between Uri and Poonch. After protracted negotiations a cease-fire was agreed to by both countries, which came into effect. Lieutenant General Kalwant Singh was not in favour of cease-fire, but Prime Minister Nehru ignored his request to capture Muzaffarabad. Both differed on Kashmir policy.

Sandhurst

Lieutenant General Kalwant Singh
It goes to Lieutenant General Kalwant Singh's credit he welded the hastily assembled units and formations into a fighting machine and with his characteristic gruff, no nonsense mannerism. He was at the same time egoistic, positively rude in speech and intolerant of inefficiency, and as a result he made a lot of enemies both within and outside the Army. He was certainly a man of iron will. He kept the force on the continuous offensive against all odds and saved two-thirds of Jammu and Kashmir for India. Lieutenant General Kalwant Singh will always be remembered as an eminent strategist and an outstanding Sikh General.

In May 1957, General S.M. Shrinagesh retired, and General Thimayya was nominated to succeed him as Chief of Army Staff, by the Prime Minister Nehru, superseding Lieutenant General Kalwant Singh, who was senior to General Thimayya. He was the second Sikh officer, the first one was Lieutenant General Sant Singh, to be bypassed and superseded to be the next Army Chief.(Incidentally Lieutenant General Sant Singh put in his papers and retired from the Army in disgust. See page 38).

His last posting was as General Officer commanding Western Command. He retired from the Army on 15TH May, 1959, and passed away on January 21ST, 1966, at Delhi.

Sandhurst

Colonel Naranjan Singh Gill
Commissioned from the RMAS in 1925
Naranjan Singh Gill was born in 1906 at Majitha near Amritsar, into distinguished family of Sir Sunder Singh Majithia. The family had provided five ADCs to five successive British Commanders-in-Chief in India. He was a natural candidate for the Royal Military Academy, Sandhurst. He graduated and was commissioned from the Royal Military Academy Sandhurst on 3RD September 1925.

Before joining his parent Regiment, the 4TH Battalion, 19TH Hyderabad Regiment, he served a year with a British Regiment, the 2ND Battalion, The Cameronians (Scottish Rifles). Then he was posted to the mounted arm of the 7TH Light Cavalry. Gill soon showed himself to be an officer of well above average ability and he graduated from the Staff College at Quetta in 1938, being selected for higher studies in Britain in 1940. But the war intervened. In April 1939 Gill rejoined the 4TH Battalion, 19TH Hyderabad Regiment at Secunderabad, where his brother officers included such later distinguished soldiers and politicians as Captain K.S. Thimayya, a future Indian Army Commander-in-Chief, and Lieutenant Mohammad Azam Khan, one day to become Prime Minister of Pakistan. Captain Gill sailed with his Regiment for Singapore in August 1939, but returned to India in December on being posted as a staff captain in Indian Army Headquarters, the first King's Commissioned Indian Officer to get a regular headquarters staff appointment.

Sandhurst

Colonel Naranjan Singh Gill
His work on the committee enquiring into Sikh unrest in 1940 so impressed the chairman, Brigadier A.E. Barstow, and the Defence Secretary that it was suggested he should be appointed to the Defence Department. When the idea was mooted there was an outcry among some of the British diehards. The unfortunate controversy, which no doubt caused some hurt to Gill, ended with a compromise solution.

He was promoted to Acting Major and posted to the staff of the 11TH Indian Division which was preparing for a move to Malaya. Gill flew out to Singapore with the advance party in October 1940. In November 1941 he was sent to Bangkok to look into the co-operative activities of the Indians and Japanese. Aware of Pritam Singh's revolutionary group, British Intelligence had in April 1941 arrested three of his agents.

These Sikhs were sentenced to ten years imprisonment by a court at Kota Bharu (but later released by the Japanese). The British also knew of Pritam Singh's links with the Shanghai Revolutionary Party, which had succeeded in converting the Granthis (priests) attached to Sikh units in Shanghai and Hong Kong. Three Granthis had been returned to India in 1941 because of their subversive work among Indian Regiments.

Gill's job entailed finding out if Pritam Singh's propaganda was having any effect on Indian soldiers in Malaya, particularly those stationed near the frontier. Gill was a good operative and he soon got to the bottom of what was going on in Bangkok.

Sandhurst

Colonel Naranjan Singh Gill

He reported back that Indian-Japanese co-operation certainly existed, but thought although the Indian militants were determined and active, they were confined to small groups; moreover, they were not making any impression at all on the Sikh soldiers. Later, Mohan Singh told Gill that until he was captured he had no idea that such a group as Pritam Singh's was at work.

The exaggerations of Pritam Singh may have been the original cause of Mohan Singh's low opinion of his colleague. Another mission, on whom Gill was employed, involved reconnaissance work in southern Thailand for the proposed 'Matador' pre-emptive operation, which the British cancelled at the last moment. After these duties, he was promoted Lieutenant-Colonel and when captured in Singapore was AAQMG with 11TH Division. On joining the I.N.A. Mohan Singh promoted him Colonel. Following the end of the war and his release from detention in the Red Fort, Delhi, by the British in April 1946, Gill immediately involved himself in Sikh political affairs, becoming President of the Combined Sikhs. In this capacity he worked closely with Gandhi and Nehru on the Sikh problems following Independence and Partition.

In the fifties he embarked on a successful career in the Diplomatic Service, and was Ambassador to Ethiopia (1955 to 1960), Thailand (1960 to 1963) and Mexico, Cuba and Panama (1964 to 1967). He lived in retirement at his family home near Amritsar.

He passed away at Amritsar on 19TH August 1992.

Sandhurst

Major General Lakhinder Singh
Commissioned from the RMAS in 1925
Lakhinder Singh was commissioned with the rank of 2ND Lieutenant on 3RD September 1925, from Sandhurst Military Academy. As was customary, he was attached to a British Battalion for a year, before being posted, initially to the 1ST Battalion, 7TH Rajput Regiment, before being transferred to the 3RD Battalion, 2ND Punjab Regiment.

When 2ND Lieutenant Lakhinder Singh joined the Battalion, it had moved from the North-West Frontier to down-town Karachi, where it remained on training and garrison duties until 1931. The next move took the Battalion back to the Frontier, this time to Wana in Waziristan. The two years spent in Waziristan were uneventful, although they naturally provided untrained officers and men with invaluable knowledge and experience of Frontier conditions. This knowledge was soon to be tested in a practical manner, for in December 1932 the Battalion was posted to the Nowshera Brigade, and subsequently took part in the Mohmand operations of 1933 and 1935 and the Loe Agra operations of the latter year. After the final action the Battalion found itself back in Nowshera by 5TH November. It remained there until 3RD March 1937, and then moved up once again to Landi Kotal. At the end of 1937, the Battalion moved from Landi Kotal to Lucknow, and was still stationed there at the outbreak of the Second World War.

In the Second World War the Battalion served in the Indian 5TH Infantry Division.

Sandhurst

Major General Lakhinder Singh

The Indian 5TH Infantry Division, comprising only two brigades at the time, was sent from India to the Sudan to reinforce the British forces there under Lieutenant-General Sir William Platt.. The 5TH Division started to arrive in the Sudan in early September 1940 and absorbed Platt's three British Infantry Battalions and formed a third Infantry Brigade. After these rearrangements, the Division consisted of the 9TH, 10TH and 29TH Indian Infantry Brigades. The Battalion formed part of the 29TH Indian Infantry Brigade. For the next three months the Division was involved in a series of aggressive skirmishing operations to keep the Italian forces off balance and confused as to Platt's longer-term intentions. In early 1941, Platt's forces were further augmented by 4TH Indian Infantry Division, rushed from the Western Desert. An attack was launched into Eritrea on 18TH January. The climax of the campaign was the Battle of Keren, a fiercely fought series of engagements against superior numbers which ended with victory for Platt's forces on 1ST April. After Keren, 4TH Indian Division was withdrawn to Cairo and 5TH Indian Division continued the campaign in Eritrea, finally joining up with elements of Lieutenant-General Alan Cunningham's forces, which had advanced north from Kenya to capture Italian Somaliland and the Italian capital of Addis Ababa in Ethiopia, to take the surrender of Prince Amedeo, Duke of Acosta, the Italian Viceroy, at Amba Alagi, and so far as further fighting was concerned the East African campaign was over.

Sandhurst

Major General Lakhinder Singh

The 29TH Indian Infantry Brigade was detached from the 5TH Indian Division and moved to the Western Desert, and was destroyed on 28TH June 1942 during the fighting at Fuka during the First Battle of El Alamein.

In August the remnants of the Battalion were collected at Mena; and for some time there seemed to be danger of its being disbanded and amalgamated with another Punjabi Battalion, as it seemed to be impossible to draw on trained reinforcements in sufficient numbers to build up to strength. However, there was a timely arrival of a large batch of reinforcements. Lakhinder Singh described these as the roughest and most ill-trained reinforcements the Battalion had ever seen; yet they responded to training sufficiently well to play their part later in the jungles of Burma and Java.

The 5TH Indian Division was moved back to India in 1943; the 3RD Battalion, 2ND Punjab Regiment, which had recently been converted to a machine-gun Battalion, arrived at the Regimental Centre at Meerut in May of that year. The Battalion then moved to Burma to face the Japanese. Japan invaded Burma in 1942, and then part of the British Empire, beginning what was to become the longest continuous campaign fought by the British during the war. It was fought in some of the most challenging terrain in the world, in a tropical climate that claimed many men before they had a chance to fight. It involved some bitter fighting that prevented a Japanese invasion of India.

Sandhurst

Major General Lakhinder Singh
From the victory in the Arakan sector the Indian 5TH Infantry Division was air-lifted to the central front. 161 Brigade joined XXXIII Corps, which was beginning to arrive at Dimapur, and fought in the Kohima. While the remainder of the Division reinforced IV Corps, whose land victory at Kohima and Imphal, in which the Division played an important part, proved to be the turning-point of the Burma Campaign.

In February 1945 Lieutenant Colonel Lakhinder Singh was appointed to command the Battalion, however, Lakhinder Singh's tenure was brief, for he was detached very shortly on staff duties. He was responsible for the administrative, operational and logistical needs of its unit. The duties included providing bi-directional flow of information between a commanding officer and subordinate military units.

Except for one period of rest and reorganization, the Indian 5TH Division continued to fight and to advance throughout the rest of the war, and took part in the final thrust by IV Corps down to Rangoon. After service in Burma the Division was the first unit to be landed in Singapore as part of Operation Tiderace and was later sent to Java as part of the Allied occupation of the Dutch East Indies. It saw heavy fighting during the Battle of Surabaya in November 1945. The Battalion's embarrassing and highly unprofitable duties in Java ended finally on 5TH May 1946, when it left Surabaya for India.

Sandhurst

Major General Lakhinder Singh

In August 1947, at the Independence and Partition of the subcontinent the 2ND Punjab remained as part of the Indian Army. Lakhinder Singh was promoted to the rank of Brigadier and given the command of HQ Jullundur Subarea.

Immediately after the partition, and the conflict between India and Pakistan over Kashmir, Brigadier Lakhinder Singh commanded the 'Zebra Brigade. By capturing Jhangar on 24TH December 1947, the raiders gained considerable advantage for building-up their forces for attacks on Naushera, Rajaori and Punch. Recapturing Jhangar thus became vital for us. The main trial of strength took place on 6TH February 1948, when the enemy attack on Naushera was decisively repulsed. This paved the way for the recapture of Jhangar on 18TH March 1948, in which the Zebra Brigade played a significant part. At the end of the hostilities, Major General Lakhinder Singh was General Officer Commanding Bengal, Bihar and Orissa Area.

(Despite desperate efforts I have not been able to obtain the date of Major General Lakhinder Singh's retirement from the Army and the date of his passing away)

Sandhurst

Major General Tara Singh Bal
Commissioned from the RMAS in 1926
Sardar Tara Singh Bal was born on 15TH August 1905, in the village of Chak in Lyallpur District, Punjab (Now in Pakistan). He grew up and studied in Chak, till he joined the Indian Army. He was selected to do his officer training at the Royal Military Academy at Sandhurst. Having graduated from Sandhurst on 4TH February 1926 as a 2ND Lieutenant, he was initially posted to a British Regiment for a year, before joining the 7TH Light Cavalry. At that time the Seventh was stationed on the North-West Frontier Province of India, where the rebellious tribesmen lived and skirmished in a constant state of unrest. The frontier proved and excellent training ground, and made all the more realistic by live bullets liberally fired by tribal snipers as well as frequent hit-and-run raids. Occasionally full scale military operations had to be mounted to bring the situation under control.
The Regiment left Dera Ismail Khan to Bolarum (Secunderabad) where it was stationed till 1929, and then moved to Sialkot, where it took part in Northern Command manoeuvres in the Pabbi Hills Gujrat (Now in Pakistan), and on termination of the manoeuvres, moved to Jullundur where it stayed till October 1933.
In October 1933 the Regiment again moved to the North-West Frontier, this time to Loralai, completing the route march of 550 miles in six weeks. The movement of baggage over such a long distance proved quite a problem for Captain Tara Singh Bal, who was then the Quartermaster.

Sandhurst

Major General Tara Singh Bal

In October 1935, the Regiment moved from Loralai back to Bolarum. The move was made from Karachi to Bombay and proved quite a novel experience for the men. From Bombay the Regiment move by road to Bolarum, where it stayed for four years, and was engaged in manoeuvres and in the Field Sports and Trick Riding.

On the eve of the Second World War, most of the senior King's Commissioned Indian Officers (KCIOs) and Indian Commissioned officers (ICOs) were posted to Staff appointments, where their seniority and experience was greatly needed due to the rapid expansion of the Indian Army. And thus the Seventh, which had started the war as one of the three 'Indianised' Regiments of the Indian Cavalry, entered the war largely officered by British officers. These officers gave the Regiment its much needed professional experience.

The last mounted parade took place in 1940, but by early 1941 the only mechanical transport the Regiment possessed were an Austin Car for the commandant and a few motorbikes for dispatch riders. Vehicles trickled in and finally a full complement of 52 Stuart tanks was received by April 1943. The Regiment was attached to the 254TH Indian Tank Brigade, in November 1941.

The major units of the Brigade, under the command of Brigadier Reginald Scoones, consisted, when it moved to Imphal in November and December 1943, of the: 7TH Light Cavalry, 3RD Carabineers, 3RD Battalion, 4TH Bombay Grenadiers.

Sandhurst

Major General Tara Singh Bal

The Brigade fought with the 5TH Indian Division and the 7TH Indian Infantry Divisions in Burma and was involved in the Battle of Imphal, Battle of Kyaukmyaung Bridgehead, Battle of Meiktilla, and the Rangoon Road. In August 1945 it was selected to form part of the British Indian Division, which was to form part of the British Commonwealth Occupation Forces of the Allied Occupation Forces in Japan. The move to Japan occurred in March/April 1946. They returned to India in August 1947.

The main party of the Regiment arrived as one body at Ranchi in August 1947. Lieutenant Colonel Tara Singh Bal took over the command of the Regiment from Lieutenant Colonel Wigram, who then became Second-in-Command pending retirement.

By this time the situation in the Punjab had deteriorated considerably, and the authorities called for the Seventh, and en route to the Punjab, Lieutenant Colonel Tara Singh Bal left the Advance Party on promotion and appointment to the command of 19TH Infantry Brigade at Agra. On 18TH September, Major Rajindar Singh joined the Regiment at Ambala Cantonment and assumed command. As a result of the partition of the Indian Army between India and Pakistan, a certain number of Regiments were allotted to each country, and in the case of mixed units, Squadrons and Companies were exchanged.

Sandhurst

Major General Tara Singh Bal

In the case of the Seventh, there was a clean exchange of Squadron with the Regiment going to the newly created Pakistan Army, as the Seventh was allotted to India.

It was at this stage that the Jammu and Kashmir Campaign opened, leading the Seventh for further distinguished service and glory.

Major General Tara Singh Bal, after commanding the 19TH Infantry Brigade at Agra, he was appointed the General Officer Commanding Delhi Area in 1948 & 1953 and Theatre Commander Jammu and Kashmir for four years from 1949 to 1953.

He retired from the Indian Army as the Quarter Master General in 1957. After retirement he was appointed as the Alternate Delegate on The International Control Commission in Laos and Saigon. He was later appointed as India's Ambassador to Argentina with accreditation to Paraguay and Uruguay.

On return he was the President of the Indian Ex Services League from 8TH May 1972 to 15TH October 1977. He took an active part in the development of Defence Colony in New Delhi, being the President of the Association from 1969-74 and 1975-78 and the founder President of the Defence Colony Club. He passed away on 4TH December 1991.

'A Marriage across Frontiers'

In August 1947, during the chaos of Partition, a young Captain Mahdi Hasnain (Joe) received a personal letter.

Sandhurst

Major General Tara Singh Bal

It was from Raza Hussain, Esq, his father in law 'to be'. Raza Husain, Esq, was the father of Miss Zakia Husain, the 20 year young girl to whom Joe was engaged to be married. Raza Husain Saheb had decided to migrate to Pakistan. Of all cities where he had found a job befitting his status was in a college at Peshawar. The family had already moved and the letter was to inform him about this. So what would happen to the wedding which was supposed to take place immediately after his arrival in India from the operations in Indonesia? Now there was an international border between them and none too friendly border. Indian troops had already landed in Srinagar and the two nations were in an awkward state of war.

Captain Mahdi Hasnain immediately went to inform his Commanding Officer, Lieutenant Colonel Mclean about his predicament. In a five minute chat with the CO it was amply clear that there was no way that Joe could go to Pakistan or get his fiancé back across the border without official sanction. Doing anything such as getting to Pakistan unofficially was ruled out due to the prevailing tensions and the roads still being jammed with refugees and ongoing communal clashes.

Then began the year with long communications between the unit and the higher headquarters on one of the most awkward situations that the 'A' Branch of that headquarters may have ever handled; the impending wedding of a young diehard Garhwali Captain and a formerly Indian and now Pakistani young lady and no solutions could be found.

Sandhurst

Major General Tara Singh Bal

No system of visas had yet been introduced and even passport control between India and Pakistan was not in place. Staff officers and commanders up and down the chain were befuddled by the awkward situation and no one was willing to take decisions. It was perhaps time to call of the engagement and move on; political events sometimes dictate destinies of a personal kind and perhaps the time had come to take a decision.

Lieutenant Colonel Mclean gave the final decision. Joe Hasnain would be given leave with a blank leave application and a Demi Official letter to GOC Delhi Area, Major General Tara Singh Bal. The letter would outline every effort made by the Unit to assist Captain Joe Hasnain and the unfortunate outcome. A plea would be made to assist the young Captain in any way the General Officer felt appropriate. It was not sure whether Lieutenant Colonel Mclean personally knew Major General Tara Singh Bal, but clearly the spirit of positivity was prevailing and this was the last ditch attempt. Joe Hasnain arrived at HQ Delhi Area at 0730 hr in the morning of 9TH August 1948; clearly the fate of his life would be decided in the next few days. He did not have to wait long because the GOC also arrived early. After perusing Lieutenant Colonel McLean's letter Major General Bal paused, reflected upon his own past (three generations in the Army). He was a Cavalryman and old world in his values. What he saw in the eyes of the young Captain standing before him was sheer sincerity.

Sandhurst

Major General Tara Singh Bal

It was his own value system which seemed to reflect from those eyes. He was sincere to his fiancé; once a decision made in life he was not going back on it until every option was exhausted. The brief interview confirmed exactly what the General had perceived; this was not an ordinary man; he was the type who would stay with his men till the last round was exhausted. That is how old time General Officers assessed their subordinates, body language was enough. General Bal spoke slowly. "Son, you are a man of your word and you belong to one of the finest units of the Indian Army; from me you won't get No as an answer. I will ensure everything in my powers to see how you can travel to Pakistan to get married and return proudly with your wife." Everywhere it was his ramrod straight gait, sincere eyes and the word of Major General Tara Singh Bal which carried the day. The good General rang up the Pakistan Army GHQ, exchanged pleasantries with old friends from the cavalry, regaled a few with his jokes and pleaded for a little help.

Finally, on 16TH August Captain Joe Hasnain was called to the office of the GOC who personally handed him three tickets to Peshawar with instructions that he had four days in which to get married and return. No leave certificates, no movement orders, everything was based upon the trust that the GOC could perceive in the personality of the young Captain. Take a relative along with you he said and ask my ADC to get you a trunk call to Peshawar to convey the message of your arrival.

Sandhurst

Major General Tara Singh Bal
The triumphant young Captain called up his elder sister's husband in Lucknow to reach Delhi at the earliest and the two flew on 18TH August 1948 direct to Peshawar. There were no entry and exit formalities even though Joe carried signals of authority for his move issued by the Pakistan Army. We need to remember that the two Armies were still officially at war. No one questioned him or asked him to stay back in Pakistan. On 19TH August 1948 he was married to Zakia, his fiancé of three years.

On 20TH August, Captain and Mrs Hasnain flew back with two suitcases. That was the dowry she brought, one suitcase of clothes and a head full of memories. For a young girl who had left India under stressful circumstances it was a grand return to Palam airport in the company of her tall and handsome husband.

Joe Hasnain went on to be a Major General, the first Muslim to command a Division in the Indian Army and retired with his chit in the pocket (cleared for Lieutenant General but not promoted due to age).

It was Major General Tara Singh Bal whose large heartedness and ability to grasp a situation ensured that our family came into being. He was the grandfather of my colleague and good friend Lieutenant General Dalbir Singh Sidhu.

Lieutenant General Syed Ata Hasnain
Indian Army

(Info supplied by Lieutenant General (Retd) Dalbir Singh Sidhu).

Sandhurst

Major General Digamber Singh Brar, OBE
Commissioned from the RMAS in 1926
Sardar Digamber Singh Brar was born on January 25TH 1905. He was in the first batch of the 'Prince of Wales Royal Indian Military College', Dehradun. From there he went to Military Academy Sandhurst, in England. He graduated from the Academy and was commissioned on 30TH August 1926, as a 2ND Lieutenant.
(It would be worth mentioning here that he was six months senior to Field Marshal Ayub Khan in Sandhurst. The Field Marshal was later also the President of Pakistan.) As was the then practice, he was attached to a British Unit, the Warwickshire Regiment for a year, after which he joined the 5TH Royal Marathas on 6TH December 1927. He took over as the first Indian Adjutant of the Battalion from 1ST January 1932.
He was then posted to command the affiliated company of his Battalion in the Training Centre, and became the first Indian Adjutant there. He held this appointment from 13TH December 1936 to 7TH April 1939. From there he attended the Staff College course at Quetta in 1940. From the Staff College he was posted as a Staff Captain to 21ST Indian Infantry Brigade, part of the famous 8TH Indian Division. He rejoined his Battalion as the Second–in–Command in 1942. The Battalion was then part of 21ST Infantry Brigade, which fought some actions in Iraq, Persia and Syria. The Persia-Iraq region, which later went under the name of 'Paiforce' which eventually, became the largest British base for military operations launched in North Africa: Western Desert and Italy.

Sandhurst

Major General Digamber Singh Brar, OBE

In 1943 the Battalion converted to Machine Gun-cum-4.2 inch Mortar Battalion, as a supporting arm for the Division and part of the Divisional troops; and moved to Italy. The campaign in Italy put Indian troops to severest test as they were pitted against the German paratroopers. Digamber Singh Brar took over as the Commanding Officer of the Battalion in 1943 and remained in command till the end of the war. He was the first Indian to get Command of a fighting unit in a war theatre.

In mid-November 1943, after crossing Biferno and Trigno rivers, the 8TH Army was closing on Sangro River. The Germans had built the strongest defences on this river known as Winter Line which ran across the waist of Italy starting from Adriatic coast. By the end of June1944, the 8TH Army had turned their attention to capture of Arezzo and Florence, as they were essential administrative and operational bases for attack on Gothic Line.

The Italian campaign had kept four Maratha units, $1/5^{TH}$, $3/5^{TH}$, $5/5^{TH}$ Royal sand 4TH Maratha Anti-Tank Regiment committed to nonstop fighting for 20 months. It was one battle after another, over mountains and rivers which had turned into most powerful bastions of defence by German forces who knew that these offered their last chance of survival. In the 200 years history of the Maratha Light Infantry, this was by far the longest campaign that Maratha soldiers fought against a modern and well organised enemy. The spring offensive of 15TH Army Group commenced in April 1945.

Sandhurst

Major General Digamber Singh Brar, OBE
The 8TH Army was instructed to go on an offensive by breaking through Senio defences.
One Sepoy, the sole survivor, was able to recross the river to give information: a soldier named Namdeo Jadhav. Namdeo after reaching far bank of the river and being the sole survivor, assumed personal command of the battle and in the midst of crashing of mortar bombs and the sweeping fire of machine guns, he nonchalantly carried two of his wounded comrades to safety through deep waters in the minefield. He dashed back to nearest German post and silenced the crew with bursts of Tommy gun and used all the grenades he had. He charged and wiped out two more German posts. Namdeo Jadhav was deservingly awarded the Victoria Cross for his outstanding bravery. It was the first ever awarded to the Maratha Light Infantry.
Digamber Singh Brar was mentioned in Dispatches in September 1944 and was decorated with the O.B.E. (Order of the British Empire) in April 1945, in recognition of gallant and distinguished service.
He moved back to India with the Battalion in July 1945. On return from active service he commanded 3RD Battalion 5TH Maratha Light Infantry and the 4TH Battalion 5TH Maratha Light Infantry for a year each. He returned to London (U.K.) for a short time to Command the Indian Contingent in the Victory Day parade held on 8TH June 1946. In June 1947 he took over 114 Infantry Brigade at Naushera (near Rawalpindi).

Sandhurst

Major General Digamber Singh Brar, OBE

In 1947 the circumstances called the formation of a peace-keeping force in Central Punjab before the announcement of a boundary award. Accordingly, on 22ND July 1947 the Partition Council authorized the setting up of a special military command for this purpose. It was to function from 1ST August and would be under the command of Major General Rees. The special force, with Headquarters at Lahore, came to be known as the Punjab Boundary Force. His charter of duties gave him the operational control of forces of both Dominions allotted to his command and he was responsible for the two Governments through the Supreme Commander and the Joint Defence Council. Brigadier Digamber Singh Brar of India and Brigadier Mohammad Ayub Khan (later Field Marshal and President of Pakistan) were appointed advisers to General Rees.

After this he was posted as the first Indian Commander of Bombay Sub Area on 1ST October 1947. He took over Bombay Area as a Major General on 4TH May 1948. A few months later in September 1948 took part in the Hyderabad police action. He controlled the entire Western boundary skirting the state, and personally led his force into Aurangabad. Major General Brar entered the Daulatabad Fort on the afternoon of 14TH September. The whole operation was over in four days and that ended the rule of the Nizam, thus annexing the State of Hyderabad into the Indian Union.

Sandhurst

Major General Digamber Singh Brar, OBE
On 1ST June 1951 appointed as GOC 25 Infantry Division in Rajaori – Poonch area and was there till 9TH November 1953, and GOC Delhi Area in November 1953.
From 10TH July 1955 to December 1957 he was the Alternative Delegate to the ICSC (International Control and Security Committee) in Indo-China and also Commander of Indian troops located there and subsequently moved as the leader of the Indian delegation and Chairman of the ICSC in Cambodia. He returned to India in December 1957. In the meantime he had retired from service on 23RD September 1955 and was re-employed while still with the ICSC. He finally retired on 8TH February 1958.
For his services to the Maratha Group he was unanimously selected to be the First Indian Colonel of the Regiment, on 1ST April 1949. He completed 10 years as the Colonel of the Regiment on 1ST April 1959, when in accordance to the rules and regulations handed over the appointment to his successor Lt. Gen. Henderson Brooks. He did not take up any job after retirement and led a quiet, happy retired life with his family. He passed away on 29TH November 1997.
(Info supplied by the General's son, Lt. Gen. (Retd) TPS Brar).

Sandhurst

Major General, Mohindar Singh Chopra
Commissioned from the RMAS in 1928

Sardar Mohindar Singh Chopra was born in Amritsar in 1907. He did his schooling at the Prince of Wales Royal Military College at Dehra Dun before being selected for Sandhurst. He was from one of the first batches of King's Commissioned Indian Officers of the Indian Army, having graduated from the Royal Military College at Sandhurst in England on August 30TH 1928. After first attachment with the 1ST Royal Fusiliers at Ambala and Kasauli, he transferred to the 1ST Rajputs before becoming the first Indian Officer to join the famous 6TH Royal Battalion of the 13TH Frontier Force Rifles at Hanguin 1932. He thus became a Piffer (the elite Frontier Force) of the Army.

When he joined the Battalion, it was on active duty on the North West Frontier Province of India. Although there were no serious operations, the Frontier was in a state of perpetual unrest, owing to the activities of political agitators, and this necessitated constant vigilance on the part of the military authorities.

In October 1936, the Battalion moved to Thal and thence by route march Razmak, to mount operation against the Faqir of Ipi. Faqir of Ipi had been inciting the tribesmen in the Lower Khaisora for some time, and efforts were made to induce the Tori Khel Wazirs to expel him or put an end to his activities. They admitted their responsibility, but professed themselves unable to control the Faqir and his supporters. It was, therefore, decided to take action against the Faqir.

Sandhurst

Major General, Mohindar Singh Chopra

The advancing troops were strongly opposed by the tribesmen, that the fame and standing of the Faqir of Ipi was well established. The mistakes made in the direction of these operations, that the gallantry of the troops could not redeem the results of the day.

During this period propaganda and hopes of loot engendered by exaggerated stories of the Khaisora fighting had induced some 500 Afghan tribesmen to come over the border and into Khaisora valley. These did not have a very happy time as they were attacked in the villages in which they sheltered and by night were shelled by howitzers from Damdil. After constant attacks the tribesmen appeared to be sufficiently chastened, that the extra troops which had been drafted into Waziristan for the operations were now withdrawn. The situation in Waziristan detrioted seriously in 1937 and extra reinforcements from India were brought into Waziristan.

Many years were spent on active duty on the North West Frontier Province before he was selected to become the first Indian Officer for the Advance Course of the Army School of Physical Training at Aldershot in England.

He graduated from the Staff College at Quetta in 1941 and served both with the Iraq-Persia (Paiforce) and in the Burma Theatre during the Second World War.

Fearful for the security of British interests in Iraq (mainly oil supply), G.H.Q. India Command was instructed by the British government to send an expeditionary force to Basra as allowed under a treaty.

Sandhurst

Major General, Mohindar Singh Chopra

The initial force comprised two brigades from the 10TH Indian Infantry Division, which secured Basra and drove up to Baghdad to meet an ad hoc force called 'Habforce' which had invaded Iraq from Palestine. Baghdad was entered by British troops on 31ST May 1941, and an armistice signed.

On 8TH June 1941, British forces invaded Syria to overthrow the Vichy French government in Syria and Lebanon. Elements of the 10TH Indian Infantry Division and 'Habforce' were used in this campaign, together with Australian, Indian and British troops from Palestine.

The Vichy French surrendered on 12TH July 1941. On 26TH August 1941, British forces invaded Persia, a sovereign country, in order to secure the country against German influence. The Persia premier agreed to a ceasefire on 28TH August 1941, although some armed resistance continued. On 1ST September 1941, British forces met up with Russian troops which had invaded Persia from the north. Persia and Iraq were then garrisoned in order to open up a supply route to Russia and to guard against German invasion through the Caucasus Mountains in early 1943. This threat quickly evaporated in mid 1943, so Persia and Iraq Command was gradually run down during the rest of the war. On the conclusion of the operations in Persia and Iraq, Mohindar Singh Chopra went on to serve in the Burma theatre. British Empire forces peaked at around 1,000,000 land, naval and air forces, and were drawn primarily from British India.

Sandhurst

Major General, Mohindar Singh Chopra

The campaign had a number of notable features. The geographical characteristics of the region meant that factors like weather, disease and terrain had a major effect on operations. It was also the only land campaign by the Western Allies in the Pacific Theatre which proceeded continuously from the start of hostilities to the end of the war. The climate of the region is dominated by the seasonal monsoon rains, which allowed effective campaigning for only just over half of each year. This, together with other factors such as famine and disorder in British India and the priority given by the Allies to the defeat of Nazi Germany, prolonged the campaign and divided it into four phases: the Japanese invasion which led to the expulsion of British, Indian and Chinese forces in 1942; failed attempts by the Allies to mount offensives into Burma, from late 1942 to early 1944; the 1944 Japanese invasion of India which ultimately failed following the battles of Imphal and Kohima; and, finally, the successful Allied offensive which reoccupied Burma from late-1944 to mid-1945.

In 1946 he was promoted to Lieutenant Colonel and took over as the first Indian Commanding Officer of the 1ST Assam Regiment in Shillong. In late 1947 he took over command of 123RD Infantry Brigade at Amritsar, charged with the onerous responsibility of not only defending hundreds of miles of turbulent frontier but also of evacuating safely nearly two million refugees during the partition of the sub continent.

Sandhurst

Major General, Mohindar Singh Chopra
In late 1949 he was promoted to Major General and given the responsibility to resurrect the famous 5TH Infantry Division, then scattered along most of north and eastern India. The 5TH Division was built up into a formidable fighting force and mobilised twice for the border crisis of 1950-51. In 1950 he was given the singular honour of being appointed Colonel-in-Chief of the 5TH Royal Gurkhas Rifles (Frontier Force) being then and remaining the senior Piffer in the Sub-Continent. In 1953 he took over as GOC 20TH Infantry Division, the last Division to have troops stationed in Tibet. Retiring from the Army in 1955 he became India's first Ambassador to the Republic of the Philippines, a post he held until 1959. On return to India, and few years of civilian life, he was appointed the Director, National Institute of Sports at Patiala, a post he held until 1968. Major General Mohindar Singh Chopra passed away in 1990.

Colonel Gurdial Singh
Commissioned from the RMAS in 1929
Sardar Gurdial Singh was commissioned from Sandhurst on 31ST January 1929, with the rank of 2ND Lieutenant. He was immediately posted to the Indian Electrical and Mechanical Engineers. By 1946 he had achieved the rank of Major. At the Division of the army in 1947 he was posted to the HQ Southern Command, India (Poona)

(In spite of repeated efforts I have been unable to obtain the information about the Colonel Gurdial Singh's consequent military service).

Sandhurst

Lieutenant General Mohinder Singh Wadalia
Commissioned from the RMAS in 1929

Lt. Gen. M.S. Wadalia was born on November 30TH, 1908, at the village of Wadala Sandhuan in Daska Tehsil of Sialkot District in the Punjab. He got his education at Royal Indian Military College, Dehradun. He was commissioned from Sandhurst, England, on 31ST January 1929 and was given KCIO (Kings Commissioned Indian Officers) and posted into the 16TH Light Cavalry of the Armoured Corps. The Regiment served in the defence of the North West Frontier of India. In the Second World War, the Regiment showed its prowess in mechanised warfare by spearheading the reconquest of Burma from the Japanese. The Regiment was the first to be selected for Indianisation and among its first officer is such distinguished leader of post-independence Indian Army as Lieutenant General M.S. Wadalia.

Before becoming Chief of General Staff (equivalent to Vice-Chief of Army Staff today) he was BGS at Western Command and commanded the prestigious 1 Armoured Division in Jhansi and 15 Corps headquarters at Udhampur, and was also the Colonel of 16 Cavalry and the Deccan Horse. He also commanded Joint Services Wing from June 1951 to January 1953. He was a services squash player, a horseman and a polo player.

Lieutenant General M.S. Wadalia, (Retd) passed away on May $21^{ST,}$ 2001. He was cremated in New Delhi with full military honours. He is survived by his daughter.

Sandhurst

Major Vir Singh
Commissioned from the RMAS in 1929
Sardar Vir Singh was sent to Sandhurst Military Academy in UK for military training. He was commissioned on 31ST January 1929, and after serving a year in a British Regiment, he was posted to 1ST Battalion, 14TH Punjab Regiment, like his brother officers Sant Singh, Mahabir Singh Dhillon and Gurdip Singh Dhillon, who had also trained at Sandhurst. Initially they all served in the same Regiment on the North-West Frontier Province.

Much happened in the years spent on the Frontier; the comings and goings on courses and leaves; the annual and General's inspections; success in sports and games; competitions for Regimental and Indian Army shooting trophies; visitors; epidemics; the road protection duties and hill training was undertaken.

By this time Gurdip Singh Dhillon had attained the rank of Captain, and has been appointed as the Adjutant of the Regiment. The Regiment had scarcely settled down at Jhelum when the Mohmad operations intervened. In 1933 dissentions between the Upper and Lower Mohmands over the latter's loyalty to Government led to the former under the Haji of Turangzai invading the Gandar Valley. The Regiment had to intervene and the Gandar Valley MT Road had been built to just short of the Nahakki Pass. Failure to insist on its extension over that historic high ground was interpreted by the Upper Mohmands as weakness, and led them to truculence.

Sandhurst

Major Vir Singh

Advancing on 23RD August, two brigades, including the Regiment, reached Ghalanai next day against appreciable opposition and during the next few days cleared the locality and established the Line of Control.

Before extending the road over the Nahakki Pass, it was decided to increase the force. All officers and men on leave in India were recalled, and the depot under Lieutenant Vir Singh was left behind in Jhelum. The first operation of significance was the passage of the Nahakki Pass. The Battalion left Ghalanai and spent building the road over to Nahakki, while the enemy harassed all they could.

On the 14TH, Battalion laid a successful ambush for the enemy parties now actively sniping Wucha Jawar Camp. The sniping could be plainly heard over the ridge, and soon became very heavy. Some fourteen of the snipers bumped into No. 4 Platoon, which opened fire at twenty yards. While some fell the remainder of the enemy ran left, until ambushed at very close range by No. 2 Platoon and suffered further casualties. Five minutes later much the same was repeated by another batch of tribesmen. Both parties now moved further west until they were shot of the muzzles of Nos. 1 and 5 Platoons. This virtually ended the operation. The tribes submitted on 3RD October. The Battalion went on to mount punitive expeditions in Waziristan in 1937-38. By now Major Vir Singh had been appointed as the Adjutant of the Regiment.

Sandhurst

Major Vir Singh

Indianisation had built up so strong a cadre of Indian officers in the 1ST Battalion, that it is became obvious to officer newly raised units.

Consequently Major Vir Singh was posted to the newly raised 9TH Battalion, 14TH Punjab Regiment in 1941, for service in Burma against the Japanese. The 9TH Battalion, 14TH Punjab Regiment as a part of the 32ND Brigade of the 17TH Division, was ordered to make a reconnaissance in force on Ningtholukhong. It was decided to thrust into the village from the north east corner. Accordingly following an air strike by twelve Vengeance Bombers, two companies of the 9TH Battalion, 14TH Punjab Regiment, supported by two troops of medium tanks and eight 25TH–Pounders from Bishenpur attacked Ningtholukhong. Unfortunately the aircraft arrived forty minutes early, before the infantry were in position, so much of the value of the air-strike was lost. The Japanese were well concealed and supported by a number medium machine-guns, which the tanks were unable to locate. Without their help the attack in broad daylight across the paddy fields, was no longer viable and was repulsed. The 9TH Battalion, 14TH Punjab Regiment suffered 85 casualties, including the gallant Major Vir Singh who was killed instantly.

Major Vir Singh is commonmenrated on the Rangoon Memorial, which bears the names of men who died during the Burma Campaign.

Sandhurst

Major General Atma Singh
Commissioned from the RMAS in 1931

Sardar Atma Singh graduated from the Sandhurst Military Academy and was commissioned on 29TH January, 1931, with the rank of 2ND Lieutenant. After doing a one year's service in a British Regiment, he joined the 2ND Battalion, 1ST Punjab Regiment.

The Battalion spent practically whole of the period between the two world wars on the North-West Frontier of India. In 1937 the trouble had been started by Mirza Ali Khan, the Faqir of Ipi, who had acquired considerable influence among the Wazirs. He managed to unite the Tori Khel Wazirs, the Mahsuds and Bhitannis, normally in state of feud with each other, against the Government of India. The rising hostility manifested itself in early February, 1937, when two British officers were murdered, one in Mahsud and one in Wazir territory. These outrages were followed by many other hostile acts, which created and alarming situation. Reinforcements were called in, the 2ND Battalion with Captain Atma Singh, was hurriedly concentrated to prevent conflagration which might envelop the whole of Waziristan. Meanwhile, elsewhere in Waziristan, many incidents had taken place demanding punishment of the offending tribesmen. Punitive action had to be taken, and the 2ND Battalion, was entrusted with the task of restoring peaceful conditions. The Battalion completed the mission in restoring peace in Waziristan before returning to Multan.

Sandhurst

Major General Atma Singh

During the Second Wold War, Major Atma Singh, was posted to the Regimental Training Centre of the 1ST Punjab Regiment. During the war the Regiment raised seven new Battalions, and thus almost trebling its original number, and in consequence had to train a very large number of recruits to meet the needs of a total of twelve Battalions and four garrison companies. At the peak of the expansion in April 1943, the authorized strength of the Regimental Centre was 37 officers, 62 viceroys' commissioned officers and 4,112 other ranks, equal to the strength of an infantry brigade.

The work done by the training staff at the Centre earned such a reputation in the Indian Army, that the representatives of most of the other Training Centres, both infantry and armoured corps, visited it during 1943. These visits were tribute to the efforts of the officers and junior leaders to achieve the highest standard of efficiency.

During the Second World War, the Battalions of the Regiment served in several theatres of war against the Japanese, Germans and Italians. Six Battalions of the Regiment took their turn in keeping watch and ward on the North-West Frontier. The total casualties suffered by the Regiment during the Second World War were 5,510 and included 118 officers, 178 viceroys' commissioned officers, 5,068 other ranks and 146 non-combatants. Atma Singh ended the war with the rank of Lieutenant Colonel.

Sandhurst

Major General Atma Singh

At the Empire Victory parade in London on June 8TH, the Regiment was represented by a contingent of three viceroys' commissioned officers, twenty-nine other ranks and three followers. In 1947 the process of dividing the subcontinent along sectarian lines took place.

The northern, predominantly Muslim sections of India became the nation of Pakistan, while the southern section became the Republic of India. The Army was also divided between India and Pakistan, and the 1ST Punjab Regiment was allotted to Pakistan and the Sikh soldiers were transferred to the Indian Army.

Immediately after the Independence, Atma Singh was rushed to Jammu and Kashmir, to contain the Pakistani aggression. At the partition of Indian Subcontinent, Kashmir being a Muslim-dominant state was considered a natural part of Pakistan, although the Maharajah of Kashmir had signed an instrument of accession with India. The Army Headquarters of Pakistan planned the main invasion plan, code-named Operation Gulmarg. According to Operation Gulmarg, every Pathan tribe was required to enlist at least one Lashkar of 1,000 tribesmen. These Lashkars were to be concentrated at Baftnu, Wana, Peshawar, Kohat, Thal and Nowshera by the first week of September 1947. The Brigade Commanders at these places were to issue arms, ammunition and some essential clothing items. Each Lashkar was also to be provided with a Major, a Captain and ten JCOs of the regular Pakistan Army.

Sandhurst

Major General Atma Singh

The entire force was to be commanded by Major General Akbar Khan, who was given the code name Tariq. When the first wave of tribal warriors from Pakistan invaded the Kashmir Valley on 22ND October 1947, the kingdom of Jammu and Kashmir had not acceded to either Pakistan or India. Therefore, taking the plea that it was an internal matter, India refused to send in its troops to the Valley.

However, Maharaja Hari Singh signed the Instrument of Accession with the Indian Government on the evening of 26TH October 1947. Now was the time to react to the tribal invasion, which India did commendably, considering the short notice given to its military commanders. On October 27TH, 1947, the Indian army entered Kashmir to flush out the intruders from Kashmir. Nearly one hundred planes were pressed into service to bring troops and arms in Leh and Ladakh. The Indian soldiers fought the war at the height of 23900 feet. Lieutenant General Kalwant Singh was in overall command and ordered, Major General Atma Singh, the first Indian General Officer Commanding (GOC) of Tiger Division, to the relief of Poonch. An attempt to link up with Poonch could be made either from the south, namely, via Thana Mandi or Rajauri, or from the north via the Haji Pir Pass. Major General Atma Singh was ordered to plan for a link-up accordingly. Major General Atma Singh was further ordered to carry out Phase I (secure Pir Badesar) by October 8TH; commence Phase II (demonstrate north of Thana Mandi) by October 10TH.

Sandhurst

Major General Atma Singh
He was to concentrate in Rajauri the required force for Operation Easy by October 16TH. On October 9TH, Major General Atma Singh finalised and implemented his orders. The main operation was to commence on about October 19TH with 5TH Brigade advancing from Rajauri and securing Pir Kalewa ridge. Major General Atma Singh now detailed 19TH Brigade Group to capture Point 5732 with a view to exploit Jhhika Gali, an enemy stronghold barring the way to Mendhar and also captured its objective at 0620 hours. Then the exploitation began. The link-up with Poonch in November 1948 was a notable performance. Operation Easy resulted in capture of 800 square miles (2,100 km) of territory. Large numbers of refugees, including 10,000 Muslims were able to get away and obtain relief from the state administration. India, against the wishes of its generals, brought the matter before the United Nations. Under the supervision of the United Nations, the cease-fire was implemented on January 1ST, 1949.
Major General Atma Singh met with a fatal jeep accident in Satwari Cantonment in Jammu on September 22ND, 1949. The Indian Army honoured Major General Atma Singh by installing his bust and a memorial at Satwari Cantonment in Jammu.

Sandhurst

Major General Pritam Singh Chowdhury
Commissioned from the RMAS in 1932

Sardar Pritam Singh Chowdhury was born on 13TH February 1911. He joined the Indian Army and was commissioned on 1ST September 1932 from Royal Military Academy, Sandhurst, as 2ND Lieutenant. As was the custom at that time, he served with the British Regiment, the 2ND Suffolk Regiment for a year. He was then posted to and served with the 5TH Battalion, Sikh Regiment for a year.

The 5TH Battalion, earlier known as the 47TH Sikhs, raised in 1901, was then based in Aurangabad in the Deccan.

He was transferred to the Royal Indian Army Service Corp in 1935 and was in charge of the supply depot at Trimughury until 1937. He was then an instructor at NCOs School at Lahore until 1941. He was instrumental in raising 67 GPT Coy (abinitio) Quetta in 1942, and took this unit by road to Baghdad, a distance of approx 1800 Km, during the Anglo-Iraq war. He was promoted to the rank of Lieutenant Colonel and became in charge of Line of Control Area to Iraq in 1943. In 1945 he was made the Officer Commanding of 9TH Motor Transport Training Centre at Meerut. He was in charge of RIASC Lahore Area 1947.

The partition of India saw him promoted to Lieutenant Colonel, Indian Army. He was 21C MEO Main HQ Amritsar 1947, and was involved in the orderly migration of Hindus, Muslims and Sikhs on both sides of the border.

Sandhurst

Major General Pritam Singh Chowdhury
In September 1948 he planned the Hyderabad police action, which ended in annexing the State of Hyderabad into the Indian Union. He was deservedly promoted and held key positions in the Indian Army i.e. Brig. Adm. SC. 1949; Director of Movement and Quartering Army HQ in 1953; DDST, Army HQ 19565; DST 18TH April 1957. He was appointed Colonel Commandant of the Regiment on 5TH July 1959. He retired from the army in June 1960. He expired on 18TH June 1985, in England.

Captain Ajaib Singh
Commissioned from the RMAS in 1933
Sardar Ajaib Singh received his commission from officer training at Sandhurst, on 2ND February 1933. After serving with a British Regiment for a year, was posted to join the 5TH Battalion, 11TH Sikh Regiment. The Battalion earlier known as the 47TH Sikhs, had completed a four year tour at Aurangabad in the Deccan by early 1939, had moved in February of that year to Razmak on the North-West Frontier of India. The Battalion served with great distinction in Waziristan, particularly in the Tochi Valley Campaign of 1940. The Battalion was to amass during its two years tour in Waziristan a very respectable list of honours, including one Distinguished Service Order, two Military Crosses, two Indian Orders of Merit, and four Indian Distinguished Service Medals. The list says much for the nature of the fighting and for the spirit and courage of the troops.

Sandhurst

Captain Ajaib Singh

During the 1941 the Battalion spent the cold weather in Razmak once more, on the same strenuous routine duties as before. The Battalion moved down from Razmak to Bareli to join the 22ND Infantry Brigade of the 9TH Indian Division. The Battalion in Bareli and embarked on the 6TH April for Malaya. As regards the troops on the spot, the Battalion was in excellent order. Much had been done, when hostilities broke out, in the coming December, to absorb 480 recruits and the six young emergency commissioned officers with whom the Battalion had embarked, but the training had been restricted by the need for putting every available man on the defence works.

Equipment was still short, and the Battalion was not up to scale till a few days before the operations begun. But the troops were fit and in excellent heart, and determined to give good account of themselves.

The Battalion was engaged in the disastrous defence of Malaya, whilst many Regiments disintegrated before the Japanese onslaught, the 5TH Battalion, 11TH Sikh Regiment held together, given an objective to take, they duly did so and held at no time did the Regiment retreat, until ordered to withdraw from their position.

It was now apparent that the threat against the Kuantan area was developing from the North and on the morning of December 30 1941 the Japanese advanced via the Jabor Valley in greater strength than they had previously shown.

Sandhurst

Captain Ajaib Singh

They were engaged by our artillery and small arms fire and confused fighting continued throughout the day.

During the night of December 31ST, the rearguard was withdrawn across the river and the ferry destroyed. At that time, however, the River Kuantan was fordable in its upper reaches, a most unusual occurrence at that time of year, this seriously weakened the defence. In the meantime the Commander Kuantan Force had been ordered to hold the aerodrome till January 5TH and this had been later extended to January 10. On January 2ND, however events on the west coast and the serious threat to communications there forced the Commander 3 Indian Corps to expedite the programme.

And early on the morning of January 3RD the Commander Kuantan Force received orders to withdraw his force to Jerantut forthwith. During the withdrawal the rearguard was twice ambushed on the main road by a Japanese force, which had passed by bush tracks west of the aerodrome, and suffered heavy casualties. One infantry Battalion, 5TH Battalion, 11TH Sikhs, was still nearly at full strength. The Kuantan Force by denying the aerodrome to the enemy for a month it had greatly decreased the scale of air attack which the enemy was able to develop against the Singapore area.

That this was so was proved by the rapid increase in the scale of that attack during the month of January. It has also been ascertained from Japanese sources that heavy casualties were inflicted on them during these operations.

Sandhurst

Captain Ajaib Singh

There is little doubt that these casualties were considerably in excess of those suffered by our own troops.

However with the relentless Japanese advance, the destruction of the British formations, the Battalion had to disperse in small parties. About 200 of the men reached Singapore while the others were combined with elements from another Battalion to form a composite 5TH Battalion, 11TH Sikh Regiment. The Battalion could not hold back the Japanese tide, and on the 27TH January was ordered to withdraw to Singapore. On the main road and railway front the enemy followed the withdrawal energetically and much fighting took place. The withdrawal of the two columns required most careful co-ordination.

There was little rest for the troops. Some parties of the enemy were met and dispersed, the 5TH Battalion, 11TH Sikh Regiment again distinguishing themselves, but the dense jungle proved too much for the troops who were hampered by having to carry a number of wounded. In spite of a continuous march of three days and nights they were unable to catch up and efforts to locate them by ground and air patrols failed.

The final withdrawal on the night of January 30TH-31ST was carried out without incident, and with little interference from the enemy's Air Force. At 8:15a.m. January 31ST all troops had been withdrawn and a gap of 70 feet was blown in the Causeway. It is estimated some 300 bridges were destroyed or damaged during the campaign.

Sandhurst

Captain Ajaib Singh
The Retreat in Malaya lasted ten weeks in far more trying conditions. There was no strong ally to help, and no Navy to evacuate the force, even had it been desirable to do so. It has been hailed as a disaster but perhaps the judgement of history will be that the effort and money expended on the defence of Malaya and the sacrifice and subsequent suffering of many of those who fought in the Malay campaign were not in vain. The gain of ten weeks and the losses inflicted on the enemy may well have had a bigger influence than was realised at the time on the failure of the Japanese to reach even more important parts of our Empire.

When Singapore fell in February 1942 the remnants of the 5TH Battalion, 11TH Sikh Regiment became POWs alongside Captain Ajaib Singh. Captain Ajaib Singh was executed in Singapore by the Japanese.

'The short campaign was over and for causes beyond our control had ended in defeat. The Battalion when given an objective to take took it; when given a position to hold, held it; in no instance did the Battalion withdraw from any position until ordered to. They proved not unworthy of the proud traditions handed on them by their predecessors.'

(Birdwood)

Sandhurst

Lieutenant Balwant Singh
Commissioned from the RMAS in 1933
Sardar Balwant Singh was commissioned from Sandhurst, UK, on the 2ND, February 1933. Having served a year with a British Regiment, he was posted to 4TH Battalion, 19TH Hyderabad Regiment.

The Regiment has had an enviable record of service in China (1900-1901), East Africa (1914-1915), Afghanistan 1919 and Iraq (1923-1924). In 1936, Lieutenanant Balwant Singh moved to Secunderabad from Quetta, with his Regiment, where it was involved in relief operations after a massive earthquake had caused untold damage and destruction.

In August 1939, the Regiment sailed for Singapore, as part of 12TH Indian Infantry Brigade. Singapore Island lies at the tip of the Malayan peninsula and is linked to the mainland with a strong causeway. The Regiment trained for jungle warfare at various locations on the Malayan peninsula. They learnt to move silently in primary jungles. However, in secondary jungles a path had to be cut to allow movement. This invariably made a lot noise and progress of troops was slow. Sometimes it took a whole day to advance a mere 10 km.

On 8TH December, there were reports of Japanese landings in Kota Bharu and 12TH Indian Infantry Brigade was ordered to hold advancing Japanese forces, from hastily prepared defensive positions near Kota Bharu. Allies realized the enemy advance had to be halted at all costs. The Regiment arrived at Krai during the early hours of 9TH December and moved to Ketereh.

Sandurst

Lieutenant Balwant Singh

The Allies tried to slow down the enemy advance by demolishing bridges and larger culverts, but the wily enemy quickly threw up improvised foot bridges and continued their rapid advance.

The Regiment was ordered to occupy a defensive position at Ketereh. During the night of 9TH December, forward troops kept falling back in disarray.

There was little rest for the troops, who remained nervous and expected Japanese forward elements to show up at any time. First contact was made with the advancing Japanese, and the situation quickly became confused. The Japanese fire was erratic and did not cause much damage. The troops remained jittery in the darkness and each company thought it was either being outflanked or attacked. As quickly as they had appeared, the enemy faded away, and the attacks ceased.

On 11TH December, it was an action filled night and the intense fire-fights took place, as the enemy made repeated attempts to assault the bride-head over Kelantan River. Each time, the enemy attacks were beaten back with casualties. Troops fought tooth and nail, and did not permit the Japanese to break into the bridge-head. The fight went on all night, with the remainder brigade providing fire-support from across the river. During the early hours of the morning, intense fire suddenly broke out from three sides, but all the enemy attempts to gain a foot-hold, were effectively foiled. On the 14TH December orders were received to occupy south bank of Nal River at Sungei Nal.

Sandurst

Lieutenant Balwant Singh

The Regiment held a six mile long frontage for the next two nights, and prevented the enemy from making either a crossing or any move along the Nal River in boats.

However, the Japanese built up along Kroh-Kuala Kangsar Road was so quick, that 12TH Indian Infantry Brigade was ordered to withdraw at midnight. A defensive position was taken at Chemor, on 24TH December 1941. The brigade met with as disaster at Chemor, and the Regiment was ordered to withdraw to Goping. During the withdrawal, the Regiment beat back two Japanese attacks and inflicted casualties. The mauled enemy pulled back and did not attempt to interfere with the Regiment's withdrawal to Slim River. After the grim fighting at Slim River, the remnants of $4/19^{TH}$ Regiment moved to Singapore, along with 12TH Indian Infantry Brigade.

On 18TH January 1942, the Regiment was ordered to prepare defences on the north end of Singapore Island, overlooking the Causeway. Since the Causeway was the only link with the Malayan peninsula, its defence was considered vital, till all the troops had been withdrawn from the mainland. On the morning of 31ST January, troops who were preparing defensive positions, watched the blowing of the Causeway. It was an awesome sight. After the massive explosions, water rushed through the 70 feet gap and Singapore Island was de-linked from the Malayan peninsula.

10TH February, Japanese aircraft bombed the Regiment and explosions ripped through the area.

Sandurst

Lieutenant Balwant Singh

Soon, a column of enemy tanks smashed through the defences and the Japanese infantry began to pour through the gap. There was destruction all round and most places were in flames. By 12TH February, the remnants had fallen back to the outskirts of Singapore City, where the Regiment suffered severe casualties. For Fortress Singapore, the end came quickly, as Lieutenant General Percival signed and unconditional surrender on 15TH February 1942 and together with Singapore garrison of 70,000 men, and the remnants of 4TH Battalion, 19TH Hyderabad Regiment passed into captivity. Regiment personnel were disgusted by the sudden turn of events that had changed their status from proud soldiers to lowly prisoners. They felt let down by events, ever since the fighting had begun. The Regiment had fought gallantly and suffered heavy casualties during the campaign in Malaya. Though heavy losses had been inflicted on the enemy, the men were surprised to see the Japanese as their captors.

The Indian prisoners of war were given the option by the Japanese to join the Indian National. Almost 40,000 Indian soldiers in Malaya did not join the army and remained as POWs. Many were sent to work in the Death Railway, and nearly 11,000 died under Japanese internment.

When Lieutenant Balwant Singh refused to join the INA, he was shipped from Singapore to a labour camp in Borneo. Here he was cruelly tied to a tree and bayoneted to death, for a minor infringement of camp rule.

Sandhurst

Brigadier Kulwant Singh Sandhu
Commissioned from the RMAS in 19232
Kulwant Singh Sandhu graduated from Sandhurst on February 2ND 1923, was commissioned with the rank of a 2ND Lieutenant. He was posted to the 5TH Battalion, 8TH Punjab Regiment. Since December 1923, 5TH Battalion 8TH Punjab had seen continuous service in Baluchistan and the North-West Frontier Province. They arrived at Jamrud in 1935, and in 1937, they were posted to Kohat, yet another frontier station. In April 1938, the Battalion moved to Spinwam in Tori Khel country in support of Tochi Scouts, who were having some trouble with the tribesmen.

In early 1940, the 5TH Battalion, 8TH Punjab were again engaged in operations against Mehr Dil in the Ahmedzai Salient. By May, the outlaw band was dispersed and the Battalion moved back to Kohat. In October 1940, 5TH Battalion, 8TH Punjab moved to Razmak.

On 31ST January 1941, the Battalion moved to Ahmed Khel in the Tochi Valley, where it was engaged operations against the Datta Khel tribesmen. This was the last operation of 5TH Battalion, 8TH Punjab on the Frontier during which they suffered several casualties. On 29TH August, the Battalion returned to Razmak, and in October, it left the Frontier for Secunderabad. Soon afterwards he was posted to RIASC and attained the rank of Brigadier.

(After desperate efforts, I could not find Brigadier Kulwant Singh's military history during his service in the RIASC and his retirement).

Sandhurst

Colonel Rajinder Singh Kalha
Commissioned from the RMAS in 1932
Sardar Rajinder Singh Kalha was born on 13TH June 1910 at Maymo, Burma. He had his early education at St. Xavier's College, Calcutta. Thereafter he joined the Prince of Wales Royal Indian Military College, Dehra Dun in 1923. On 28TH January, 1932, he was commissioned from the Royal Military College, Sandhurst, and was attached with the Dorset Shire Regiment for a year. In Waziristan in March 1933, he was posted to the Indian Army in the, 14TH Punjab Regiment and remained on military duty up to 20TH November 1937.

He joined the Survey of India at Dehra Dun on the 25TH November 1937 as an Assistant Superintendent, in which post he was confirmed with effect from 21ST November, 1939. After completion of his training at Dehra Dun, he was posted to "A" and "E" Companies in Frontier Circle, Murree (now in Pakistan) where he remained up to 1942, and holding charge of various units. On 14TH October, 1942, he was mobilized for active service and commanded an Indian Field Survey Coy., R.I.E., which actively participated in the Defence of Imphal, during the Japanese invasion down the Manipur Valley. He was "Mentioned in Despatches" for Service in Burma in 1945.

The following medals were awarded to him: The North West Frontier 1936-37, the 1939-45 Star, The War Medal 1939-45, The Indian General Service 1939-45, The Burma Star, and the Independence Day 1947.

Sandhurst

Colonel Rajinder Singh Kalha

After Second World War, he took charge of No.18TH (Air Survey) Party at Risalpur, on the 16TH December 1945. He was then transferred to Calcutta and appointed as Deputy Director, Map Publication with effect from 1ST March1946. He assumed the duties of Deputy Director, Eastern Circle at Calcutta with effect from 1ST March, 1947. He was promoted as Major with effect from 1^{S} July 1947. From the 16TH December 1947 to the 1ST January 1948, he officiated as Director, Eastern Circle. On the 24TH February1948, he was again reverted to Military duty and was appointed as Deputy Director, Military Survey, Geographical Section, General Staff Branch, Army Headquarters, in the rank of Colonel. While on Military duty, Colonel Kalha was appointed in the grade of a Director, Survey of India, from 18TH May, 1948, in which post he was with effect from 2ND December, 1949.

In April 1952 and was posted as Director, Eastern Circle, Shillong, Calcutta. He was transferred to hold the post of Director, Map Publication, Dehra Dun, with effect from 30TH November, 1955, which post he held till promoted Surveyor General of India on the 1ST May1961. He reverted to his substantive post of Director, Map Publication on 11TH December, 1961 and took premature retirement from service with effect from 1ST February 1966. Colonel Kalha also officiated as Surveyor General for short spells from 1ST December 1958, to 14TH February, 1959, from 1ST December, 1959 to 28TH February 1960 and from 12TH December 1964 to 13TH January, 1965.

Sandhurst

Colonel Rajinder Singh Kalha

Colonel Kalha was an excellent officer with sound knowledge and experience of Surveying, Drawing and Map Reproduction. He was keen on modernizing the techniques and so kept himself informed by studying the latest literature on various subjects, evincing interest in Scribing. He was conscientious, hard working and a very capable administrator. He was excellent in planning and guided his officers on sound lines. Colonel Kalha was a fine and thorough gentleman, just and extremely kind. He was popular with all ranks.

After retirement, he settled down on his farm near Sonepat (Haryana), where he devoted his time to his hobbies i.e. amateur radio communication and agriculture.

His wife, Ardaman, belonged to the well known Bagrian family of Punjab. Of his five daughters three were married to military officers and one to a naval officer, who all rose to the ranks of general officers.

One of his younger brothers, Lieutenant Colonel Sarbjit Singh Kalha, was from the first batch of the Indian Military Academy. He was commissioned in the 1ST Sikh Regiment and was awarded DSO and Bar while commanding his Regiment during the War. He was killed in an ambush by the Japanese the day he was to leave for home. Colonel Rajinder Singh Kalha passed away on July 2ND 1974, at Delhi.

(Info supplied by Amrita Harwant Singh, daughter of Col. RS Kalha)

Sandhurst

Lieutenant General Bikram Singh PVSM
Commissioned from the RMAS in 1932

Bikram Singh was born on July 4TH 1911 in the village of Kahma, district Jullundur. He came from a famous military family of Punjab. His father Narain Singh had an illustrious career in the army. Risaldar Major Honorary Captain Narain Singh had earned the IDSM for gallantry and was awarded the OBE. He had the privilege to be one of the few to be selected as ADC to King Edward V111 during the years 1932-1935.

Bikram Singh got his education from Prince of Wales, Royal Military College, Dehradun, India. He was selected for training at Royal Military Academy Sandhurst. After graduation from Sandhurst he was commissioned in 1932. He was then attached for one year to 6TH Royal Berkshire Regiment, a British Battalion.

He was then posted to 6TH Battalion, 13TH Frontier Force Rifles at Kohat, on the North-West Frontier of India. In October 1936, the Battalion moved from Kohat to Thal and thence marched to Razmak. Bikram Singh saw action against the Faqir of Ipi. The Faqir had been inciting the tribesmen in the Lower Khaisora for some time, and efforts were made to induce the Tori Khel Wazirs to expel him or put an end to his activities.

The Jirgah admitted their responsibility, but professed they were unable to control the Faqir and his supporters. It was therefore decided to take military action against the Faqir and his supporters. The initial British action at Khaisora met with a reverse.

Sandhurst

Lieutenant General Bikram Singh PVSM

During this period propaganda and hopes of loot engendered by exaggerated stories of the Khaisora fighting induced some 500 Afghan tribesmen to come over the border and into the Khaisora Valley. They did not have very happy time, as they were constantly attached while advancing and later in the villages in which they had taken shelter. The fighting was too much for the Afghan tribesmen, most of them returned to their own country. Various Jirgah were now held, and the tribesmen appeared to be sufficiently chastened, and the British put an end to the operations against them.

The situation in Waziristan deteriorated seriously during the early months of 1937, and had to be dealt with, and this the Battalion did very professionally.

After taking part in various operations in the North-West Frontier Province, Bikram Singh, during the Second World War, served for sometime in the desert of North Africa as well as in Iraq and Iran.

During the war, the British Forces numbered 36,000 in Egypt and 8,000 in Sudan. These were faced by 215,000 Italians to the west in Libya and 250,000 in East Africa. The latter had invaded Sudan from the east, forcing the British to evacuate Gallabat and Kassala, and were threatening to advance on Khartoum.

But the Italian High Command were over-cautious and in the event it was British numerically inferior force that struck first, and the Battalion took a lion's share in the fighting in Sudan and Eritrea. Bikram Singh had fought actions in Egypt, Libya, Iran, Iraq, Syria and Palestine.

Sandhurst

Lieutenant General Bikram Singh PVSM
Then after his outstanding military service, he was hauled back to India, and transferred Rajput Regiment. He was sent to the Staff College at Quetta. Subsequently, he held a staff appointment with the famous 26TH Infantry Division in the Far East.

The 26TH Indian Infantry Division saw fighting in the Burma Campaign. When the Japanese invaded Burma in 1942, the various units in training or stationed around Barrackpur near Calcutta were hastily formed into the "Calcutta" Division on 20TH March 1942. On 15TH May, the Division was retitled the Indian 26TH Division. The Division's badge was a Bengal tiger stepping through a blue triangle, representing the "delta" of the Ganges River, on a black background. For much of 1942, the Division was heavily engaged in internal security. It formed part of Indian XV Corps, but late in 1942, it was taken over directly by Eastern Army. For the First Arakan offensive, all the Division's brigades were detached one by one and committed to the offensive under the 14TH Indian Infantry Division. In March, the offensive stalled and the HQ of 26TH Division relieved that of the 14TH Division, taking over the Arakan front too late to prevent a minor disaster. After this the British fell back almost to their starting point on the Indian frontier.

Once reorganised, the Division was in reserve for the first part of the Second Arakan Offensive, once again under XV Corps. When a Japanese counter-attack at Ngakyedauk cut off the forward troops, 26TH Division was deployed to relieve them.

Sandhurst

Lieutenant General Bikram Singh PVSM

It fought down the coastal plain to reopen the roads by which the 5TH Indian Division was supplied. After the battle ended with the repulse of the Japanese attackers, the Division took over the 5TH Division's front and took part in the capture of two vital railway tunnels After this, the Arakan offensive wound down to spare troops and resources for the battles in Manipur. The Division was withdrawn during the monsoon rains to recuperate.

Beginning in late 1944, the Division was committed once again to the Arakan. During the Third Arakan Offensive and subsequent operations, 26TH Division took part mainly in amphibious operations, including the unopposed capture of Akyab Island, and the Battle of Ramree Island. Finally in April and May 1945, the Division took part in Operation Dracula, the capture of Rangoon. At the Japanese surrender, the Division, reinforced other troops in Java and Sumatra, where the end of the war brought widespread disorder. The Division was formally disbanded in India on 31ST August 1945, but most of its units were stationed in Sumatra at Padang and Medan until November 1946, when they embarked at the port of Belawan for India.

In 1947, Bikram Singh was in command of the 4TH Battalion the Rajput Regiment. The British were going to hand over the reins of the country, but unfortunately the country was divided into two, India and Pakistan. The partition of the country was calamitous. The partition of the subcontinent rendered millions of people homeless.

Sandhurst

Lieutenant General Bikram Singh PVSM

The Government had to set up refugee camp to provide shelter to the homeless at various places. One such camp perhaps the biggest of its kind was set up at Kurukshetra. At that time, Bikram Singh had attained the rank of Colonel and was chosen for the job and was posted to the refugee camp at Kurukshetra. In 1948, he was promoted to the rank of Brigadier. He was given the command of an Infantry Brigade in Jammu and Kashmir. Later on he was posted to Assam where he served till 1953.

After that, he was appointed staff officer in charge Administration of Eastern Command. In August 1955, he was promoted as Major General and was in command of a Division in Jammu and Kashmir. Then he was sent to Assam and was appointed as General officer commanding. He was responsible for restoring law and order in the turbulent Naga Hills. After that he was posted as General Officer Commanding Delhi and Rajasthan area. In 1961, he was selected to command a Corps in the rank of Lieutenant General.

During the Chinese aggression in 1962, he performed a miraculous job in saving Ladakh from the Chinese. He provided effective and competent leadership and thus the Chinese were stopped in their tracks.

His tactics and strategy went long way to save Ladakh from the hands of the enemy. While on the Eastern Front the Indian soldiers got drubbing under General Biji Kaul. The Kashmir Front under Lieutenant General Bikram Singh was able to drive out the Chinese from Ladakh. No doubt, he came to be known as 'Hero of Ladakh'.

Sandhurst

Lieutenant General Bikram Singh PVSM

In spite of reverses in North East, there was mood of victory in Ladakh and this was due to men like Lieutenant General Bikram Singh who without adequate weapons and equipment went ahead, otherwise it was clear that in Ladakh same fate would have awaited as on the Eastern Front. On 16TH November 1963, he was promoted to the rank of Army Commander, Headquarters Western Command. He was to take over command on December 3RD 1963, from Lieutenant General Daulat Singh. But during his last visit to the forward areas in Jammu and Kashmir sector on 22ND November 1963, the cruel hand of fate cut a promising career short. The General along with General Daulat Singh and four other senior officers were killed in a helicopter crash near Poonch. Lieutenant General Bikram Singh was honoured by the Government of India and was awarded PVSM posthumously.

He was so popular with the government of Jammu and Kashmir and the Chief Minister Jammu and Kashmir rang up Prime Minister Jawaharlal Nehru and in a voice choked with emotion requested him to permit the dead body of General Bikram Singh to be taken for cremation in Jammu and Kashmir.

The 10 feet long bronze statue of the late General Bikram Singh PVSM at Bikram Chowk in Jammu is a living monument of his sacrifice for Jammu and Kashmir and the love of the people for him.

Sandhurst

Major Mahabir Singh Dhillon
Commissioned from the RMAS in 1924

Sardar Mahabir Singh Dhillon was sent to Sandhurst Military Academy in UK for military training. He graduated from the Academy and was commissioned 27TH August 1924, and after serving a year in a British Regiment, he was posted to 1ST Battalion, 14TH Punjab Regiment, like his brother officers Sant Singh, Gurdit Singh Dhillon and Vir Singh, who had also trained at Sandhurst. Initially they all served in the same Regiment on the North-West Frontier Province.

Much happened in the years spent on the Frontier; the comings and goings on courses and leaves; the annual and General's inspections; success in sports and games; competitions for Regimental and Indian Army shooting trophies; visitors; epidemics; the road protection duties and hill training was undertaken.

By this time Mahabir Singh Dhillon had attained the rank of Captain, and has been appointed as the Adjutant of the Regiment. The Regiment had scarcely settled down at Jhelum when the Mohmad operations intervened. In 1933 dissentions between the Upper and Lower Mohmands over the latter's loyalty to Government led to the former under the Haji of Turangzai invading the Gandar Valley. The Regiment had to intervene and the Gandar Valley MT Road had been built to just short of the Nahakki Pass. Failure to insist on its extension over that historic high ground was interpreted by the Upper Mohmands as weakness, and led them to truculence.

Sandhurst

Major Mahabir Singh Dhillon

They refused to hand over certain outlaws; they quarrelled with the Lower Mohmands over the distribution of the road contract money; and finally in mid-August they started to demolish the road. Their Lashkar at first numbered 1,400 Burhan Khel and Isa Khel, but soon greatly increased from the Safis and other tribes.

Advancing on 23RD August, two brigades, including the Regiment, reached Ghalanai next day against appreciable opposition and during the next few days cleared the locality and established the Line of Control. Before extending the road over the Nahakki Pass, it was decided to increase the force. All officers and men on leave in India were recalled, and the depot under Lieutenant Vir Singh was left behind in Jhelum. The first operation of significance was the passage of the Nahakki Pass. The Battalion left Ghalanai and spent building the road over to Nahakki, while the enemy harassed all they could.

On the 14TH, Battalion laid a successful ambush for the enemy parties now actively sniping Wucha Jawar Camp. The sniping could be plainly heard over the ridge, and soon became very heavy. Some fourteen of the snipers bumped into No. 4 Platoon, which opened fire at twenty yards. While some fell the remainder of the enemy ran left, until ambushed at very close range by No. 2 Platoon and suffered further casualties. Five minutes later much the same was repeated by another batch of tribesmen. Both parties now moved further west until they were shot of the muzzles of Nos. 1 and 5 Platoons.

Sandhurst

Major Mahabir Singh Dhillon

This virtually ended the operation. The tribes submitted on 3RD October. The Battalion went on to mount punitive expeditions in Waziristan in 1937-38. By taking part in the Waziristan operations the Battalion earned another clasp to the Indian General Service Medal.

During the Second World War, the Battalion fought in the Malayan Campaign. In December 1941, a small mechanized force advanced into Siam from north of Kedah to harass and delay the advance of the Japanese forces from Singora. An armoured train was also sent into Siam from Padang Besar on the frontier of Perlis. By dusk on 9TH January, 1942, the mechanized force halted at Sadao, ten miles north of the frontier on the Jitra-Singora road. A Japanese column, headed by tanks and moving in close formation with full headlights, was seen approaching. The leading enemy tanks and a convoy of some thirty motor vehicles behind them were engaged and brought to a standstill; but the Japanese Infantry quickly debussed and started an enveloping movement. Thereupon, the mechanized force withdrew southwards towards the frontier, destroying Road Bridge as it went. It passed through 1ST Battalion, 14TH Punjab, who had been detailed both to provide the covering troops on the frontier and to hold an outpost position three and half miles north of Jitra.

Early on the morning of 10TH, the Japanese made contact with forward detachments of 1ST Battalion, 14TH Punjab, which had been providing both the covering and outpost troops of this sector.

Sandhurst

Major Mahabir Singh Dhillon

The Punjabis withdrew slowly southwards. Meanwhile, to give sufficient time for 15TH and 6TH Brigades to prepare and occupy their allotted sectors, General Murray-Lyon instructed Brigadier Garret to delay the enemy north of Jitra till dawn on 12TH, and gave him 1ST Gurkha Rifles to assist him. Garret ordered this unit to take over the outpost position at Asun and concentrated the whole of 1ST Battalion, 14TH Punjab forward.

On 11TH, enemy infantry attacked and in the fighting, the defence lost some ground and the two Breda anti-tank guns. Since the whole of the Battalion was to delay the enemy without becoming too involved, Garret had decided to withdraw it during the afternoon through the outpost position at Asun, but Murray-Lyon ordered him to occupy an intermediate position near Nangka, some two miles north of the outpost position and to hold it overnight. The Punjabis were moving to this position in heavy rain and in poor visibility when a Japanese mechanized force, led by medium tanks followed by lorried infantry, suddenly attacked the rear of the column. Firing indiscriminately ahead and to both sides, the tanks broke through the rearguard and drove through the column, overrunning the section of 2ND Anti Tank Battery which was limbered up and not in action. They caused utter consternation among the Indian troops, most of whom had never seen a tank. The Punjabis were thrown into confusion by this attack and forced off the road.

Sandhurst

Major Mahabir Singh Dhillon

Only some 200 men succeeded in joining the Division the following day. Small parties made their way back later but, for the time being, the 1ST Battalion, 14TH Punjab could not be regarded as a fighting unit. The British-Indian troops were compelled to withdraw from the State of Perlis.

On 24TH December, General Heath had selected two main positions suitable for defence south of Ipoh, the first at Kampar and the second north of Janjong Malim. He decided that the reconstituted 15TH Brigade, which included the 1ST Battalion, 14TH Punjab, should occupy the Kampar position. In accordance with this plan 15TH Brigade, now rested and partly re-equipped, had moved to Kampar position on 23RD and had begun preparing defences. The 15TH Brigade, with 88TH Field Regiment and 273RD Anti-Tank Battery under command, was disposed in considerable depth astride the trunk road at Kampar Village.

The Japanese lost no time in attacking the Kampar position. The 11TH Indian Division managed to delay the Japanese advance at Kampar for a few days, in which the Japanese suffered severe casualties, in terrain that did not allow them to use their tanks or their air superiority, to defeat the British. However, the British were compelled to withdraw their troops, and the 15TH Brigade withdrew to Sungai. Apart from the air reconnaissance on both coasts of the Peninsula, little direct air support was available for British troops throughout this critical period.

Sandhurst

Major Mahabir Singh Dhillon

The relentless Japanese advance compelled the remnants of the 1/14TH Punjab to retreat to Singapore. The Japanese Army invaded the island of Singapore on 7TH February and completed their conquest of the island on 15TH February, capturing 80,000 more prisoners out of the 85,000 allied defenders.

'The Indian National Army' (INA) consisted mostly of Indian prisoners of war who had been captured by the Japanese in the course of service in the British Indian Army. On 17TH February 1942 one of the prisoners, Captain Mohan Singh of the 14TH Punjab Regiment, was appointed as leader, and he called upon the Indian prisoners to form an army to free India. While a prisoner of war, Mahabir Singh Dhillon joined the 'The Indian National Army'.

INA unit was sent to Burma under the leadership of Colonel Gill. Gill had been commissioned at Sandhurst and had experience in intelligence for the British Army in Bangkok before the outbreak of hostilities in the Pacific. Gill's assignment was to send specially trained men into India for intelligence and propaganda. Once the Japanese-INA force was prepared to enter India, Gill's team was to foment anti-British sentiment among the Indian troops. Gill's party split into two groups, one operating in the Chin Hills near Imphal, the other in the Akyab sector. Gill had already discussed escape possibilities with another Sikh officer, his friend Major Mahabir Singh Dhillon.

Sandhurst

Major Mahabir Singh Dhillon
He now chose three more Sikh officers in Singapore and recruited thirty Sikh soldiers.

He then sent the party through Kalewa under Major Dhillon, to reconnoitre routes into India. The Dhillon party left Rangoon by train and then pushed to North Burma by elephant.

Dhillon reported to an Indian Army unit at Tamu on October 5TH, with vital information about the INA, the day of arrest in Arakan of Gill's genuine spy rings of which Dhillon knew nothing, and was followed by eleven more escapers in November. The capture of the Arakan party had aroused Japanese suspicions. Before Gill found it safe to accompany his remaining escapers, he was summoned to Singapore and arrested. He spent the rest of the war in Japanese prison. Mohan Singh then dissolved the INA and resigned. He too was put under arrest.

Major Mahabir Singh Dhillon spent the rest of his days, in the service of the Sikh Panth (Sikh community).

Malaysia

With Lieutenant Colonel Baldev Singh Johl (Retd), Malaysian Armed Forces

The Sikhs came to Malaysia 160 years ago in two groups, the earlier as British prisoners in Malacca and Singapore and latter as policemen for the Straits Settlements. Many of the prisoners in Malacca and Singapore settled there after completing their sentences and formed the first Sikh settlements in these areas. The first batch of policemen arrived in Malaya in 1873. They were employed in the Perak Armed Police to keep order in tin mines, then riddled with gang fights. The Sikhs were chosen by the British because of their excellent record of service in the Sikh Regiments in India. They served well and many died on duty. Their excellent service here prompted requests for more personnel and their number soon increased. Kedah was the first Unfederated Malay State to employ Sikh Sepoys in 1883, and other states followed suit. Scattered Sikh communities soon grew in other areas of the Peninsula. A close knit community grew and the foundation was set for a further increase in the Sikh population. By the 30s and 40s, first generation of Malaysian Sikhs was beginning to grow up and the Sikh population was thriving and beginning to play a more active role in society. When the new nation 'Malaysia' was formalised on 16TH September 1963, the Sukarno regime of Indonesia declared a state of confrontation against Malaysia. President Sukarno had in mind a different federation, one comprising Indonesia, the Philippines, together with Malaya and British Borneo and vowed to destroy Malaysia.

Malaysia

During the confrontation period, the war once fought from scattered bases by sections and platoons against infiltrators became a more demanding company commander's war against Indonesian regulars on enemy soil. The confrontation lasted for four years; a communist uprising in Indonesia and growing economic difficulties which called for rapprochement with neighbours made a continuation of confrontation an irrelevance. Dr Suharto, Sukarno's successor, ended it all in May 1966. The British Defence Minister Healy referred to the campaign as *'one of the most efficient uses of military force in history'*.

This is the story of the Malaysian Sikh cadets who attended the Sandhurst Military Academy, and were commissioned into the Malaysian Armed Forces. They attained very high ranks in the Army, and true to the traditions of their forefathers, they served unconditionally, giving their best in the defence of their motherland.

(With strenuous efforts the information about Malaysian Sikh officers was obtained by Lieutenant Colonel Baldev Singh Johl (Retd),)

Sandurst

Major Lakhbir Singh Gill
Commissioned from Sandhurst in 1955
Date of Birth: 3RD November 1930
Enlisted: 11TH August 1952
Corps: Federation Regiment and Royal Ranger Regiment
Awards: GSM Malaya, UN Medal Congo, PKB and PPM

Sandurst

Major Lakhbir Singh Gill

Major Lakhbir Singh Gill was a pioneer Sikh to join the Army Service in July 1952, to attend officer training at the RMAS. He was at RMAS with another Sikh, Colonel Harchand Singh. The basis for Lakhbirs selection was to form the first multi-racial Battalion, 1ST Federation Regiment, for Malaya. It was part of the effort to unite the Malayan people in the fight against the Malayan Communist Party (MCP) during the First Malayan Emergency (1948-1960) and to prepare for Malaya's independence (1957). Major Lakhbir was trained from 10TH September 1953 and was commissioned on 3RD February 1955. He was posted to 1ST Federation Regiment as a Troop Commander. He held various appointments then on as junior officer at Regimental and formation levels that enabled him develop into a hardened field officer. From April 1961 to March 1962 he was deployed as part of the Malayan Contingent under the UN for peace keeping in the Congo. In 1964, upon the formation of Malaysia, he was transferred into the Royal Ranger Regiment where he served as the Second-in-Command of 4TH Royal Ranger Regiment from 1966 to 1968. Later, as an experienced field officer he held appointments dealing with liaison with the Royal Malaysian Air Force (RMAF) during the Second Malaysian Emergency (1968-1989). Before his retirement in 1979 he was managing defence operation at MINDEF. Major Lakhbir Singh Gill was an active sportsman having played hockey and cricket for the Armed Forces.

Sandurst

Colonel Harchand Singh
Commissioned from the RMAS in 1955
Date of Birth: 7TH April 1930
Enlisted: 8TH September 1952
Corps: Federation Regiment and Royal Ranger Regiment
Awards: GSM Malaya, UN Medal (Congo), PPA, PPM, KPK, ADK, KMN, PPT and Mention in Despatch.

Colonel Harchan Singh can be considered as one of the pioneer Sikhs to join the military service. He enlisted in 1952 and was trained initially at Eaton Hall, UK from 24TH April 1953 to 22ND August 1953 and later at the RMAS from 9TH September 1953. He was commissioned on 3RD March 1955 and posted to 1st Federation Regiment. He served with the Malayan Special Force Congo (UN) from September 1961 to December 1962. For his involvement in some local conflicts in the mission area he was awarded the *'Mention in Despatch'* in 1965. Colonel Harchand was a fieldsman and a favourite among the soldiers. He had the honour to command four of the nine Ranger Regiments: the 2ND, 4TH, 5TH, and 9TH Royal Ranger Regiments where his units had several encounters with the militant groups of the Malayan Communist Party (MCP). In all his leadership was exemplary. He had a break from active operations as Defence Attaché to Vietnam from December 1976 to January 1979. His vast experience in the field saw him being the Chief Instructor at the Army Combat Training Centre and later as its Commandant before his retirement in April 1985. He currently resides in a coastal and peaceful town of Port Dickson, some 150kms south of Kuala Lumpur.

Sandurst

Brigadier General Baljit Singh
Commissioned from the RMAS in 1955
Date of Birth: 1ST February 1933
Enlisted: 2ND February 1953
Corps: Federation Regiment and Royal Ranger Regiment
Awards: GSM Malaya, UN Medal Congo, PPM, AMN, PBS, PKB, PKM, KMN, PAT and SMP

Brigadier General Baljit Singh joined the Army on 2ND February 1953. He was first trained at Eaton Hall, UK from 29TH August 1953 to 17TH December 1953 and later at RMAS from 10TH March 1954 to 27TH July 1955. He was commissioned on 27TH July 1955 and posted to 1ST Federation Regiment. He served with the Malayan Special Force Congo Group (UN) from November 1961 to August 1962. He was awarded *'Mention in Despatch'* for outstanding actions in the Congo. After his early Regimental and staff appointments he was brought in to command the prestigious 1ST Royal Ranger Regiment from April 1971 to January 1973. The unit achieved incredible success against the communist threat in Sarawak during his tenure as its commander. His staff appointments include two spells as Defence Attaché to the Republic of Cambodia from January 1975 to January 1976 and New Zealand from October 1976 to December 1977. On his return he commanded the Rajang Area Security Command (RASCOM), a multi agency establishment combating the communist insurgency in Sarawak, East Malaysia. He was later made the Commandant of the Malaysian Army Combat Training Centre from 1st January 1981 to 31ST December 1981.

Sandurst

Brigadier General Baljit Singh

Upon a successful tour at the centre he was promoted to Brigadier General on 1ST January 1982 (the second Sikh officer to be promoted to the rank of Brigadier General (after Rajbans Singh Gill) to command the 1ST Malaysian Infantry Brigade from January 1982 to December 1983. Later set up and commanded the 10th Malaysian Infantry Brigade from January 1984 to October 1985 after which he was the Commandant of the Malaysian Armed Forces Defence College (MAFDC) from November 1985 to April 1986. He was then posted to command the 13TH Malaysian Infantry Brigade till his retirement in January 1988. He passed away in on 7TH April. 2010.

Major H Daljit Singh

Commissioned from the RMAS in 1958
Date of Birth: 11TH December 1933
Enlisted: 5TH April 1954
Corps: Electrical Mechanical Engineers
Awards: PKB, PPA and PPM

Major H Daljit Singh joined the service in 1954 and was selected to attend RMAS from 19TH September 1956. He commissioned from the academy on 1st August 1958. He was posted into the Electrical and Mechanical Engineers (EME) and was posted to the various fighting units to command Light Aid Detachment units during the period from 1958 to 1963. From 1963 to 1969 he was at 1ST Infantry Brigade as its staff officer (BEME). He retired from this appointment. In his brief spell in service, Major Daljit served with elegance and was a valuable member of the EME Corps.

Sandurst

Lieutenant Colonel Dulip Singh
Commissioned from the RMAS in 1958
Date of Birth: 23RD December 1934
Enlisted: 5TH April 1954
Corps: Service Corps
Awards: PKB, PPM, KPK, PPA

Lieutenant Colonel Dulip Singh joined the service in 1954 and was selected to attend RMAS from 19TH September 1956. He commissioned from the academy on 1ST August 1958. He was posted into the Service Corps where he held various appointments in the Transport Company in support of combat operations till 1965. He then held several appointments as logistics staff officer at formation levels to 1968 including a spell at Service Corps Directorate from 1969 to 1971. From 1971 till 1973 he was the Chief Instructor at the prestigious Royal Military College. He then held various appointments at formation level till his retirement in 1978. Colonel Dulip was a keen sportsman and played hockey for the Armed Forces. He was an outstanding member of the Service Corps.

Lieutenant Colonel Mohinder Jit Singh
Commissioned from the RMAS in 1958
Date of Birth: 3RD April 1932
Enlisted: 19TH February 1955
Corps: Engineers
Awards: KMN, AMN, PKB, PPA, PPM and UN Congo

Lieutenant Colonel Mohinder Jit Singh joined the service in February 1955 and was selected to attend RMAS.

Sandurst

Lieutenant Colonel Mohinder Jit Singh
He commissioned from the academy on 1ST August 1958. He held appointments in the Engineer Squadron before joining the Engineer Directorate as a staff officer at MINDEF. He served with the Malayan Special Force Congo Group (UN) from November 1961 to August 1962. On his return he commanded field squadron before assuming command of 1 Division Engineer Regiment in Kuching, Sarawak in East Malaysia. Before his retirement in 1977 he was in MINDEF again as a logistics staff.

Lieutenant Colonel Bhajan Singh
Commissioned from the RMAS in 1958
Date of Birth: 9TH October 1937
Enlisted: 8TH January 1956
Corps: Signals
Awards: PKB, PPA, PJK, KMN, PPM
Lieutenant Colonel Bhajan Singh joined the service in January 1956 and was selected to attend RMAS from 19TH September 1956. He commissioned from the academy on 1ST August 1958. He was posted into the Signals Corps. He held appointments as troop commander before becoming Officer in Command of 3RD, 5TH and 8TH Squadrons. Colonel Bhajan was posted as Second in Command of 2 Division Signal Regiment in Sungei Besi. He was then promoted and posted to the Armed Forces Staff College as a Directing Staff. He then returned to command 2 Division Signal Regiment before his retirement in 1975.

Sandurst

Colonel Sukhdev Singh Gill
Commissioned from the RMAS in 1958
Date of Birth: 23RD March 1936
Enlisted: 20TH July 1955
Corps: Engineers
Awards: SPI (Kelantan), PTS, PAT, PIS, KMN, PPM, SK, KPK, PPA

Colonel Sukhdev Singh joined the service in July 1955 and was selected to attend RMAS from 18TH January 1957. He commissioned from the academy on 18TH December 1958. He was posted into the Engineer Corps. He had his early baptism in the Field Squadrons as troop commander and Second in Command. His quick rise in career saw him become Brigade Major of 2ND Infantry Brigade before he was promoted to command the 1st Division Engineer Field Regiment in Kuching, Sarawak, and East Malaysia. He then held appointments as Directing Staff at Armed Forces Staff College (AFSC) and as Chief Instructor Engineer School in Kluang. He then returned to AFSC as the Deputy Commandant before assuming the post of Defence Attaché to Korea. On his return he was the Deputy Commander of 21ST Infantry Brigade before his retirement in March 1991. In his illustrious career, Col Sukhdev displayed great humility and passion in his assignments. He passed away in 2014.

Sandurst

Lieutenant Colonel Sarjit Singh
Commissioned from the RMAS in 1958
Date of Birth: 11TH November 1937
Enlisted: 8TH January 1956
Corps: Armour.
Awards: KMN, AMT and PKB

Lieutenant Colonel Sarjit Singh joined the service in January 1956 and was selected to attend RMAS from 18TH January 1957 to 18TH December 1958. He served as a troop commander in 1st Recce Regiment before doing his staff Grade 3 appointments at 2 Infantry Brigade. He then returned to 1ST Recce as a Squadron Leader. He next served as Second in Command in 2ND Recce Regiment before embarking on, to be an instructor at the Junior Staff School (Grade 3 level) in Port Dickson. He returned to command 3RD Recce Regiment before assuming the appointment of Directing Staff at the Armed Forces Staff College (AFSC). Colonel Sarjit then embarked on a series of extra Regimental appointments before his retirement in 1989. Colonel Sarjit Singh was a well-read officer who carried himself with great distinction. He was humble and very approachable to junior officers. He passed away in 1994.

Captain Akual Singh
Commissioned from the RMAS in 1962
Date of Birth: 14TH January 1941
Enlisted: 8TH December 1960
Corps: Engineers
Awards: PPA

Sandurst

Captain Akual Singh
He was commissioned into the Engineer Corps and served in 1ST Engineer Squadron in Taiping as a Troop Leader and Second in Command.
He was then posted to 10TH Engineer Squadron as an instructor before assuming appointment as Second in Command of 2ND Engineer Squadron, Taiping. He then served as Staff Officer Grade 3 Engineer Branch at Headquarters 2ND Division, Sungai Besi in Kuala Lumpur. He then retired in 1969 and migrated to Europe without further contact.

Major Sarjit Singh Sindhu
Commissioned from *the RMAS* in 1963
Date of Birth: 19TH July 1943
Enlisted: 15TH December 1961
Corps: Signals
Awards: AMN, PPA
Major Sarjit Singh Sindhu was a brilliant Signals officer who sadly passed on during a squash game while in service. He joined the service in December 1961 and was selected to attend RMAS from 9TH January 1962 to 20TH December 1963. Upon his commission he was posted into the Signals Corps. He served as the Signal Officer in 2 Federation Regiment before joining the Special Forces as the Second in Command of the Signals Squadron. He then became an instructor at the Royal Military College, Sungei Besi, and Kuala Lumpur. After which he attended an Advanced Signals Course in the US. Upon his return he assumed appointments of Officer in Command of four Signal Squadrons.

Sandurst

Major Sarjit Singh Sindhu
He attended Staff College in 1975. He next held the appointment of Grade 2 Operations at 2 Infantry Division Headquarters, a rare task for a non-infantry officer. Major Sarjit was then posted as Chief Instructor at the Grade 3 Officer Staff Course in Port Dickson. Unfortunately, he suffered a heart attack during squash game and passed away on 15TH October 1979, a sad loss of a dynamic personality. He was a great sportsman and represented Malaysia in hockey at the 1964 Olympics. He also played cricket for the Armed Forces and was an excellent golfer. He passed away in 1979.

Major Jugjit Singh
Commissioned from *the RMAS* in 1966
Date of Birth: 27TH December 1944
Enlisted: 1ST January 1965
Corps: Electrical and Mechanical Engineers (EME)
Awards: PPA
Major Jugjit Singh joined the service in 1965 and was selected to attend RMAS from 5TH January 1965 to 8TH December 1966. He was commissioned into the EME Corps and served in 1ST workshop before moving on to Kuala Lumpur Garrison as a Staff Officer. He was then posted EME School as Chief Instructor before becoming officer in Command of 2ND Workshop, in Taiping. He served in EME Directorate prior to his retirement in 1983. Major Jugjit displayed great humility and passion in his assignments. He was very popular with the lower ranks often displaying great leadership to all ranks. He passed away in 1997.

Sandurst

Lieutenant Colonel Amreek Singh
Commissioned from *the RMAS* in 1974
Date of Birth: 31ST August 1950
Enlisted: 1ST December 1972
Corps: Rangers
Awards: SSB, ABS, KAT, PJK, PPA

Lieutenant Colonel Amreek Singh joined the service in December 1972 and was selected to attend RMAS from 4TH January 1974 to 18TH December 1974. While at RMAS Colonel Amreek had the distinction to win the Sword of Honour for the best overseas cadet, an achievement not matched yet. He was posted into the Ranger Corps and served in the 1ST Ranger Regiment before serving as an instructor at the Royal Military College Sungei Besi in Kuala Lumpur. He served at several appointments at Grade 2 Staff level before assuming command of a Territorial Regiment and later the 9TH Ranger Regiment. Colonel Amreek then retired from service in 1997.

Major Harjit Singh Randhawa
Commissioned from Sandhurst in 1975
Date of Birth: 20TH May 1951
Enlisted: 14TH August 1970
Corps: Engineers and Intelligence
Awards: AMP, PPA

Major Harjit Singh Randhawa joined the service in August 1970 and was selected to attend RMAS from 5TH January 1975 to 18TH December 1975. He was posted into the Engineer Corps.

Sandurst

Major Harjit Singh Randhawa
He served as troop commander in the 15TH Engineer Squadron and 10TH Regiment.
He had a short spell with Special Forces and undertook underwater construction works during highly classified operations. In late 1985 he joined the Intelligence Corps and was again deployed for special operations. Major Harjit retired in 1995.

Major Jagjeet Singh
Commissioned from the RMAS in 1978
Date of Birth: 21ST January 1957
Enlisted: 8TH June 1976
Date of Commission: 2ND March 1978
Corps: Royal Artillery Regiment
Awards: AMP, PPA
Major Jagjeet Singh joined the service in June 1976 and was selected to attend RMAS from 8TH June 1976 to 2ND March 1978. Upon commissioning he was posted into the Royal Artillery Regiment where he served as troop commander and rose to command a Battery in 3rd Royal Artillery Regiment. He had a spell at the Artillery Directory before attending the Malaysian Armed Forces Staff College in 1988. He served in Artillery School as an instructor and later as Chief Instructor and returned to 3RD Artillery Regiment as its Second in Command where tragically passed away in office in December 1997. Major Jagjeet had the distinction of playing hockey for the Armed Forces and was a class marksman in small arms. He was a pleasant and a class of gentleman of the Armed Forces.

Indian Artillery

Historically Mughal Emperor Babur is popularly credited with introduction of Artillery in India, in the Battle of Panipat in 1526, where he decisively used gunpowder firearms and field artillery and defeated the much larger army of Ibrahim Lodi, the ruler of the large North Indian Delhi Sultanate, thus laying the foundation of the Mughal Empire.

During the reign of Muhammad Shah the empire began to break up and vast tracts of central India passed from Mughal to Maratha hands. The militant Marathas were expert horsemen who refused to engage in set-piece battles, but rather engaged in campaigns of guerrilla warfare, a war of raids, ambushes and attacks upon the Mughal supply lines. The Marathas were unable to take the Mughal fortresses via storm or formal siege as they lacked the artillery, but by constantly intercepting supply columns, they were able to starve Mughal fortresses into submission. Successive Mughal commanders refused to adjust their tactics and develop an appropriate counter-insurgency strategy, which led to the Mughals losing more and more ground to the Maratha. The Indian campaign of Nader Shah of Persia culminated with the Sack of Delhi and shattered the remnants of Mughal power and prestige, as well as drastically accelerating its decline and alarming other far-off invaders, including he later British. Many of the empire's elites now sought to control their own affairs and broke away to form independent kingdoms. In the next decades the Sikhs battled against the Mughals, only to prove the fragmented state of the empire.

Indian Artillery

The Mughal Emperor Shah Alam II made futile attempts to reverse the Mughal decline and ultimately had to seek the protection of outside powers. In 1784, the Marathas under Mahadji Scindia won acknowledgement as the protectors of the emperor in Delhi, a state of affairs that continued until after the Second Anglo-Maratha War. Thereafter, the British East India Company became the protectors of the Mughal dynasty in Delhi. After the fall of Delhi, the British had a standoff against Maharajah Ranjit Singh. Consequently they entered on a friendship treaty on 1ST January 1806, between the British and the Sikh Kingdom.

The Sikh Army was the most potent force faced by the British in India. The gunners and their pieces of artillery were the legacy of Maharaja Ranjit Singh. The Maharaja ruled the Punjab for 40 years and built the artillery of the Khalsa Fauj (Army) to an unprecedented efficiency level. No Indian ruler could match the genius of Ranjit Singh.

The period from 1801 to 1839 marked the development of the Sikh army from a semi feudal and disorganized force to an efficient fighting machine that could hold its own against the best European armies .The most lethal part of the Sikh army were the guns manufactured at the maharaja's foundries at Lahore. These guns added teeth to the Khalsa (Sikh) army making it into a formidable force. The Sikhs soon mounted an invasion of the North West. In battles with the Pathans and the Afghans in the Frontier region the Sikh Army made significant use of Artillery.

Indian Artillery

When the Maharaja died in 1839 he left behind a potent military force equipped with professional artillery.

The British, by then firmly installed in Ferozepore at the Sikh frontier, were watching the happenings across the border with more than neighbour's interest. They had been extremely farsighted in their expansion of India and wanted to extend their power to the continent's natural border, the North West Frontier. After the fall of Delhi, they had practically boxed in the Sikh Kingdom and had made no secret of their intention to destroy the Sikh Kingdom and annex the Punjab to the British Empire. With their underestimation of the fighting qualities of the Sikh soldier, the British started massing their armies; the largest force ever assembled in India, on the Kingdom's borders. The Sikh ranks, alerted to the danger of a British offensive, started their own preparations. The Sikh soldier was extremely brave and had always carried everything before him. However, the Khalsa were led by traitors. The two principal generals, Lal Singh and Tej Singh, were not Sikhs, but Brahmin Hindus, and were not committed to the cause for which they were fighting.

"A powerful, well-trained, and confident Sikh army prepared for war under the leadership of a Commander-in-Chief under orders from a Vizier, and watched from the sidelines by a powerful and clever chieftain. All three men dedicated to the defeat of the army they lead, and secretly informing their British opponents of that fact!"
(Donald Featherstone)

Indian Artillery

The battles at Mudki and Chillianwala will forever be etched in the memory of the glorious effect of the Sikh artillery while the sun was setting on the Sikh Kingdom. The guns proved their worth during the Sikh wars and many Sikh gunners were enrolled by the British in their artillery after the annexation of the Punjab.

The Indian Rebellion of 1857 was sparked off in Meerut on 10TH May 1857. Many of the Indian personnel of the Bengal Artillery were involved in the mutiny and the three Battalions of foot artillery then in existence were all disbanded in 1862. Subsequently all Indian artillery units were disbanded except for four mountain artillery batteries of the Bombay Army

In the 20TH century, the Artillery was later involved in extensive service in the First World War, in East Africa, Gallipoli, Mesopotamia, and Palestine.

The Regiment of Artillery was raised on 15TH January 1935. Originally called the 'Indian Regiment of Artillery', which later became 'The Regiment of Indian Artillery' on 1ST November 1940 and 'Royal Regiment of Indian Artillery' in October 1945, after its success in World War II.

After the partition of India in 1947 RIA was divided between the newly formed artillery Regiments of India and Pakistan. In the coming years the artillery took part in all the operations fought by the Indian Army, the latest being the Kargil War.

Indian Engineers

The Corps of Engineers is one of the oldest arms of the Indian Army. It was established in the year 1780 when the two regular pioneer companies of the Madras Sappers were raised. Subsequently, the Group of Madras, Bengal and Bombay Sappers were formed and later merged on 18TH November 1932 to form the Corps of Engineers in its present form. They were formed into field companies (a sub-unit organization that exists to this day) and grouped into Regiments.

The Indian Army Corps of Engineers consists of three major constituents namely Combat Engineers, MES (Military Engineering Service) and Border Roads. The Corps also provides officers to the Military Survey and Defence Research & Development Organisation (DRDO).

The role of Combat Engineers is to provide mobility to own forces by constructing bridges, tracks and helipads; on the other hand the Corps denies the same to the enemy by creating obstacles such as laying mine-fields and demolition of bridges.

The need for accurate survey arose before combat engineering. Vast holdings had to be carefully delineated and mapped out, to plan the correct form of commercial extraction. By 1780, serious attention began to be given to the art of sapping and mining. Forts abound in the subcontinent, and to the forts the main defences withdrew for a protracted stand. On being invested, the siege (heavy) artillery including trench mortars or bombards went at it.

Indian Engineers

The real work, not for the faint-hearted, went to the sappers who had to do the 'sapping' or mining. Sapping is the technique of accurately digging trenches, usually covered or zigzag, to cover one's approach to the point of assault.

The military engineers are mainly responsible for the design, construction and maintenance of all works, buildings, airfields, dock installations, etc. They are also engaged with additional services such as military roads, water and electricity supply, drainage, refrigeration, furniture, required by the Army, Navy and Air Force in India.

Military Engineer Services (MES) is the largest construction agency in the country. As the premier engineering arm of the Ministry of Defence, the MES primarily provides for the three arms of Defence forces, the Army, Air Force and Navy and also to other Defence related departments and organizations. It was founded in 1851 to provide rear-line-engineering support to the erstwhile British Indian Army. The Border Roads Organisation is another major arm of the Defence services which is playing a vital role by constructing national highways, airfields, buildings and bridges. The Border Roads, by constructing a large number of roads in once inaccessible areas of the Himalayas, Rajasthan and North Eastern States have contributed significantly to their economic development.

Royal Military Academy Woolwich

The Royal Military Academy (RMA) at Woolwich, in southeast London, was a British Army military academy for the training of commissioned officers of the Royal Artillery and Royal Engineers.

Woolwich

Lieutenant General Prem Singh Gyani, PVSM, OBE
Commissioned from Woolwich in 1931

Sardar Prem Singh Gyani was born on 17TH July 1910. In the competitive combined examination for admission to Sandhurst, Woolwich and Cranwell in November 1929, Prem Singh Gyani was the highest-scoring candidate and opted for the Artillery. After graduating from Woolwich he was commissioned in the Regiment of Artillery on 27TH August 1931. After serving a period of attachment with the Royal Artillery he was posted to A Field Brigade, Indian Artillery. He attended the Staff College Course in 1941. During the Second World War he served in Burma with various units and formations, and was awarded O.B.E. He was the first Indian Commanding Officer of 2ND Field Regiment, which he took over in November 1944. He led the Indian Artillery contingent at the Victory Day Parade at London in 1946. He attended the Long Gunnery Course in the U.K. in 1947. He became the first Indian Commandant of the School of Artillery when he was promoted as Brigadier in October 1947. He was also the first Indian Director of Artillery from December 1947 to December 1950. In 1951 he attended the Imperial Defence College, London. During 1952-54, he commanded 7TH Infantry Brigade and 81ST Independent Brigade Group.

Woolwich

Lieutenant General Prem Singh Gyani, PVSM, OBE
In July 1954, he was sent as Alternate Delegate (Military) to the International Commission for Supervision and Control for Indo China. Promoted as Major General in April 1955, he was appointed Commandant of the Defence Services Staff College, Wellington. He took over as the Director of Artillery in March 1959. Shortly afterwards in June 1959, he was appointed GOC of 4TH Infantry Division. He was sent as the Commander of United Nations Expeditionary Force for Gaza as a Lieutenant General in January 1960. He took over as Head of the UN Force in Cyprus in 1963, an assignment which he relinquished in July 1964. General Gyani retired from service on 3RD October 1964. He was Colonel Commandant of the Regiment of Artillery from 4TH October 1954 to 3RD October 1964. He was awarded the PVSM for his services,
Lieutenant General Prem Singh Gyani passed away at Chandigarh on 3RD June 1988.

Major General Harkirat Singh
Commissioned from Woolwich in 1932
Sardar Harkirat Singh was one of the most eminent personalities in the Corps whose contribution in shaping the future of the Corps included all facets pertaining to Combat Engineers, MES and Border Roads Organisation. As a matter of fact, the General Officer went even beyond and was responsible for laying the foundations of the Corps of Mechanical Engineers, being the first DEME. The General was a man of many talents and finest tastes both mechanical and artistic.

Woolwich

Major General Harkirat Singh

Music and Urdu poetry featured prominently in his interests and in addition he was a horticulturist par excellence and the HQ Mess gardens at the College of Military Engineering are a living testimony to his horticulturist talents.

Harkirat Singh was born on 7TH April 1911 and was commissioned into the Madras Sappers on 1ST January 1932, after his training at Woolwich, England. His first posting was to 85 Field Company in the North West Frontier Province. Thereafter, he had an extended tenure in the MES in the same region and in the Manipur-Burma sector during the Second World War. He also served a brief tenure in Japan, after which he attended the course at Staff College Quetta.

Partition of the subcontinent brought rapid promotions and he became the Chief Engineer Southern Command in December 1947 followed by the appointment as the Chief Engineer Western Command in March 1950. After having being the Chief Engineer of two Commands, he went to command an Infantry Brigade, before returning to Pune for a second tenure as Chief Engineer Southern Command. He became the Commandant of the College of Military Engineering in 1957. It was a befitting honour and a proud day for the Sappers when he was made Director of the Corps of Electrical and Mechanical Engineers in the rank of Major General. In 1960 he was appointed Engineer-in-Chief of the Indian Army, the appointment he held till he retired from the army in 1965.

Woolwich

Major General Harkirat Singh
His close association with the Corps, however, continued throughout his life and he remained Colonel Commandant till 1971.

Major General Harkirat Singh was well known not only in the Corps of Engineers and the Indian Army, but also to the Engineering fraternity in India and abroad. He was elected President of the Institution of Engineers (India) for two tenures in the early 1960's, a distinction rarely achieved.

Major General Harkirat Singh was the Chairman of the Guiding Committee which formulated the National Building College of India, a singular document in which all information and standards pertaining to construction are stipulated. It is a living memory to the eminence and foresight of Major General Harkirat Singh and till date remains a bible for all building construction activities in India. For a man of his technical eminence, retirement from the army only meant working in different spheres. In 1965, he was appointed Advisor to the Planning Commission on Housing Construction Economics and Urban Development. He was actively associated with the Hindustan Construction Company, BEML, and Hindustan Housing faculty.

Among his many achievements as Engineer-in-Chief, he was responsible for the recognition of the MES and the creation of the now commonly accepted concept of Zonal Chief Engineers.

Woolwich

Major General Harkirat Singh

It was also during his tenure that the Border Roads Organisation, which is now such an important facet of the Corps, came into being.

In recognition of his crusading zeal and valuable contribution in the field of standardization, the General was awarded the Moudgil prize in 1970.

In March 1983, Major General Harkirat Singh passed away at the Army Hospital, Delhi, after a brief illness at the age of 72. A true Sapper and Pioneer Major General Harkirat Singh was a fine gentleman, generous, hospitable and visionary. His achievements will perhaps remain unparalleled for all time to come.

The Harkirat Singh Memorial Gold Medal has been instituted by Mrs. Harkirat Singh in memory of her late husband. The medal is awarded for outstanding excellence in the Field of Engineering and is open to all the officers of Corps of Engineers, MES and Border Roads up to the rank of Colonel.

The design of Gurdwara at Hemkunt

The resultant design was a harmonious blend of crucial factors. The success of the design can also be attributed to the far-sightedness of Major General Harkirat Singh who was instrumental in suggesting several design factors with respect to the future.

Woolwich

Brigadier Anup Singh Kalha
Commissioned from Woolwich in 1933

Sardar Anup Singh Kalha was commissioned in the Royal Indian Artillery on 31ST August 1933 as 2ND Lieutenant. After serving a period of attachment with the Royal Artillery he was posted back to Royal Indian Artillery as a Lieutenant. During the Second World War he served with the 2ND Indian Field Regiment.

On 26TH May, 1942, 3RD Motor Brigade Group which included 2ND Indian Field Regiment, moved to an area south of Bir Hacheim which was held by a Free French Brigade. At six o'clock that evening, 2ND Indian Field Regiment was warned to expect an attack by armour in strength early next morning. The morning of 27TH May confirmed the previous evening's information. German armour equivalent to about two armoured Divisions could be seen in harbour 3000 yards from the Indian Motor Brigades' forward defended localities. The Commanding Officer ordered all batteries to engage the German armoured concentration. Their fire scattered the soft vehicles, while the German tanks formed up for an attack. The troops of 3RD and 7TH Field Batteries engaged the tanks at a range of 300 yards and hit some of them with their very first shots. Then the German tanks came up in greater strength. The orders were to fight to the last man and the last round.

The forward troops kept fighting the seemingly unending number of tanks. Some German armour came round the flank to attack the 4TH Battery and the rear troops. The last tank disabled by C Troop 7TH Field Battery came to a stop ten yards from No. 3 gun.

Woolwich

Brigadier Anup Singh Kalha

The gun position officer and a gun detachment commander were killed and the No 1 wounded severely. In 3RD Battery area, a shell landed in a gun pit in 'B' Troop position and killed three of the detachment. The gun was brought into action quickly and the troop knocked out another 5 tanks. 'A' Troop destroyed 7 tanks.

The performance of the Indian Artillery was praised by Mr. Winston Churchill himself on the floor of the House of Commons of the British Parliament, on the day following the action at Bir Hacheim. Kalha was decorated with the North African Star and quickly rose to the rank of Major.

The end of the Second World War brought in the Independence of the Indian sub-continent, into India and Pakistan. During the process of Independence Lieutenant Colonel A.S. Kalha, was appointed, Commander Artillery JAK force in the rank of Colonel. After the assumption of office of the Director of Artillery by Major General Prem Singh Gyani, he promoted Colonel A.S. Kalha to the rank of a Brigadier. Meantime fighting had broken out in Jammu and Kashmir between India and Pakistan.

Participation of Indian Artillery in Jammu and Kashmir operations during 1947-48 commenced with the first flights of civil and Royal Indian Air Force Dakotas, which transported 1 Sikh Battalion to Srinagar on the morning of 27TH October 1947. Personnel of 2ND Field Regiment (SP) and 13TH Field Regiment donned uniform of 1 Sikh under Captain Chauhan of 13TH Field Regt.

Woolwich

Brigadier Anup Singh Kalha

It operated as infantry till the first week of November 1947 when four 3.7 inch howitzers reached the area. Thereafter they took over the guns and assisted the infantry to drive out the infiltrators along Srinagar - Baramula road. Later artillery proved to be a battle winning factor in the defence of Srinagar airfield and subsequent route of Pakistani tribesmen in Jammu region and Kashmir Valley. Artillery played a dominant role in the recapture of Poonch, Rajauri, Thangdar, Tithwal, Dras and Kargil during 1947-48. The Chinese Army attacked Indian positions on 10TH October 1962 in the general area of Tawang in Kameng Frontier Division. Support of artillery was immediately called for, and Indian Gunners responded with gusto - notwithstanding the fact that the guns had the daunting task of reaching up to Bum La Pass in high altitude to give cover to Tawang town.

On 23RD October the Chinese came through Bum La Pass and attacked 1 Sikh position. They were immediately engaged by the guns of 7TH Mountain Battery which broke the attack. Artillery kept supporting the infantry till Tawang was abandoned. In Ladakh Sector too, artillery of 13 Field Regiment and 38 Field Battery played a significant role in holding the enemy and defending Chushul heights. Having played a significant role in these actions, he retired from the Army, having commanded the Western Command, and Command of Punjab and Himachal Area. Brigadier Anup Singh Kalha passed away in Chandigarh on 4TH July 1998.

Indian Air Force

The Indian Air Force was established in British India as an auxiliary air force of the Royal Air Force and adopted the Royal Air Force uniforms, badges, brevets and insignia. On 1ST April 1933, the IAF commissioned its first squadron, No.1 Squadron, with four Westland Wapiti biplanes and five Indian pilots.

The first five pilots commissioned into the IAF were Harish Chandra Sircar, Subroto Mukerjee, Bhopindra Singh, Aizad Baksh Awan and Amarjeet Singh. All of them were commissioned as Pilot Officers in 1932 from RAF Cranwell. Subsequent batches inducted before World War II included Aspy Engineer, K. K. Majumdar, Narendra, Daljit Singh, Henry Runganadhan, R. H. D. Singh, Baba Mehar Singh, S N Goyal, Prithpal Singh and Arjan Singh.

During World War II, the IAF played an instrumental role in blocking the advance of the Japanese army in Burma, where its first air strike was on the Japanese military base in Arakan. It also carried out strike missions against the Japanese airbases at Mae Hong Son, Chiang Mai and Chiang Rai in northern Thailand.

The IAF was mainly involved in Strike, Close Air Support, Aerial Reconnaissance, Bomber Escort and Pathfinding missions for RAF and USAAF Heavy bombers. RAF Pilots were embedded in IAF units and vice versa to gain combat experience. IAF pilots participated in air operations in Europe as part of the RAF. During the war, the IAF went through a phase of steady expansion.

Indian Air Force

New aircraft, including the U.S. built Vultee Vengeance, Douglas DC-3 and the British Hawker Hurricane, Supermarine Spitfire and Westland Lysander, were added to its fleet.

In recognition of the services rendered by the IAF, King George VI conferred the prefix "Royal" in 1945. Thereafter the IAF was referred to as the Royal Indian Air Force. In 1950, when India became a republic, the prefix was dropped and it reverted to Indian Air Force.

With the partition of the Indian sub-continent into two separate nations, the Union of India and the Dominion of Pakistan, the military forces were also partitioned. This gave a reduced Royal Indian Air Force and a new Royal Pakistan Air Force in 1947.

In a bid to gain control of the erstwhile princely state of Jammu and Kashmir, Pathan tribesmen poured into Kashmir on 20TH October 1947, aided by the Pakistani Army. Incapable of withstanding the armed assault in his province, the Maharaja of Kashmir, Hari Singh, asked India for help. The Government of India made its assistance conditional upon Kashmir's accession to India. The Instrument of accession was signed on 26TH October 1947 and the next day Indian troops were airlifted into Srinagar. The agreement was later ratified by the British.

Taking off from Safdarjung, then known as Willington Airfield, the IAF landed Indian troops at Srinagar airfield at 09:30 hours IST on 27TH October. This was the most instrumental action of the war as the troops saved the city from the invaders.

Indian Air Force

Apart from the airlifting operations and supplying essential commodities to the ground troops, the Indian Air Force had no other major role to play in the conflict. On 31ST December 1948, both nations agreed to a UN mediated cease-fire proposal marking the end of hostilities. A Line of Control has since separated Indian-held Kashmir from Pakistani-held Kashmir.

In 1962, border disputes escalated into full-scale war between India and China. Indian military and civilian leadership failed to organise and co-ordinate the air assaults efficiently and eventually the Indian Air Force was never used during the conflict apart from occasional supply missions.

Three years after the Sino-Indian conflict, India went to war with Pakistan again over Kashmir. Learning from the experiences of the Sino-Indian war, India decided to use its air force extensively during the war. This was the first time the IAF actively engaged an enemy air force. However, instead of providing close air support to the Indian Army, the IAF carried out independent raid missions against Pakistani Air Force (PAF) bases. These bases were situated deep inside the Pakistani territory, making IAF fighters vulnerable to anti-aircraft fire. On 1ST September 1965, the IAF fighters intervened in an ongoing battle between Indian and Pakistani forces in Chhamb. However, it was inadequate in close air support roles. Initially, IAF had sent the obsolete Vampires and later Mystères to stop Pakistani advance. But after incidents of friendly fire, they were not called again for close air support.

Indian Air Force

Two days later, IAF Folland Gnat fighters shot down a PAF F-86 Sabre over Chhamb area. The Gnats were effective against the F-86 and earned the nickname Sabre Slayer. According to one Western source, the Gnats accounted for at least 6 Sabre kills.

During the course of the conflict, the PAF enjoyed qualitative superiority over the IAF because most of the jets in IAF's fleet were of World War II-vintage. Despite this, the IAF was able to prevent the PAF from gaining air superiority over conflict zones. By the time the conflict had ended, both sides claimed victory in the air war; Pakistan claimed to have destroyed 104 aircraft against its own losses of 19, while India claimed to have destroyed 73 enemy aircraft and lost 35 of its own. Despite the intense fighting, the conflict was effectively a stalemate. More than 60% of IAF's air combat losses took place during the disastrous battles over Kalaikunda and Pathankot. However, the IAF lost most of its aircraft on ground and the attrition rate (losses per 100 sorties) of the IAF stood at 1.49 while PAF's attrition rate was 2.16, because the IAF had a larger number of aircraft with a higher number of takeoff and landing sorties.

After the 1965 War, the Indian Air Force went through an intense phase of modernisation and consolidation. With newly acquired HF-24, MiG-21 and Sukhoi Su-7BM (though the versions of these acquired between 1965 and 1971 did not have night-flight capability) aircraft, the IAF was able to measure up to the most powerful air forces in the world.

Indian Air Force

The professional standards, capability and flexibility were soon put to the test in December 1971 when India and Pakistan went to war over (then) East Pakistan. At the time, the IAF was under the command of Air Chief Marshal Pratap Chandra Lal. On 22ND November, ten days before the start of a full-scale war, four PAF F-86 Sabre jets attacked Indian and Mukti Bahini positions near the Indo-Bangla border in the Battle of Garibpur. In what became the first ever Dogfight over East Pakistan skies (present day Bangladesh), three of the 4 PAF Sabres were shot down by IAF Gnats, and hostilities commenced. 3RD December saw the formal declaration of war following massive, but failed pre-emptive strikes by the Pakistan Air Force against the Indian Air Force installations in the west. The PAF targets were against Indian bases in Srinagar, Ambala, Sirsa, Halwara and Jodhpur on the lines of Operation Focus. But the plan failed miserably as Indians had anticipated such a move and no major losses were suffered. The Indian response over Pakistan skies however produced severe blows to the PAF. Within the first two weeks, the IAF had carried out more than 4,000 sorties in East Pakistan and provided successful air cover for the advancing Indian army in East Pakistan. IAF also assisted the Indian Navy in sinking several Pakistani naval vessels in the Bay of Bengal. In the west, the air force demolished scores of tanks and armoured vehicles in a single battle - the Battle of Longewala. The IAF pursued strategic bombing by destroying oil installations in Karachi, the Mangla Dam and gas plants in Sindh.

Indian Air Force

As the IAF achieved complete air superiority over the eastern wing of Pakistan within a few days the ordnance factories, runways, and other vital areas in East Pakistan were severely crippled. In the end, the IAF played a pivotal role in the victory for the Allied Forces leading to the liberation of Bangladesh. In addition to the overall strategic victory, the IAF had also claimed 94 Pakistani aircraft destroyed, with some 45 of their own aircraft admitted lost. The IAF had however, flown over 7000 combat sorties on both East and West fronts and its overall sortie rate numbered over 15000. Comparatively the PAF was flying fewer sorties (though PAF had qualitative advantage; its Mirage III fighter/bombers could fly at night, where no IAF fighter had that capability—the only aircraft in IAF with this capability was the Canberra bomber) by the day fearing loss of planes. Towards the end of the war, IAF's transport planes dropped leaflets over Dhaka urging the Pak forces to surrender; East Pakistani sources note that as the leaflets floated down, the morale of the Pakistani troops sunk as they surrendered

The Sikhs have been pioneers in flying, be it in military or civil aviation, as pilots or engineers, virtually from the dawn of flight. Sikhs remain at the forefront of aviation activities be it with the Indian Air Force, Naval Air Arm, Army Aviation Corps, or the air wings of the Coast Guard and Border Security Force. The Royal Air Force Museum London presents an exclusive opportunity to view a documentary on Sikh fighter pilots, directed by Navdeep Kandola.

Indian Air Force

"Flying Sikhs - A History of Sikh Fighter Pilots" provides an intimate portrait of the Sikh pilots who contributed so valiantly to British success in World War I and World War II. The history of the Sikhs who flew in the Royal Flying Corps, the Royal Air Force and the Indian Air Force has been forgotten, yet their bravery was recognized widely by both the military and the public during the dark days of the Blitz and the brutal Japanese invasion from the East. Drawing on interviews with the last remaining pilots, rare and personal archive materials, and unseen footage, Flying Sikhs pays testimony to the brave and selfless contributions these unsung heroes made to the war efforts across the world. The dramatic and often emotional documentary reveals the pioneering role that Sikhs have played in both introducing and sustaining aviation in India. It was a Sikh - the Maharaja of Patiala, Bhupinder Singh - who procured the first Bleriot monoplane and Farman biplanes in 1910. The first ever Indian pilot to try to enlist as a pilot in WWI was Hardit Singh Malik.

Hardit Singh Malik was the only Indian pilot to miraculously survive the war and later went on to become PM of Patiala and High Commissioner to both Canada and France. The documentary includes firsthand accounts taken from the only TV Interview of Sardar Malik and a rare interview with his daughter Harji Malik. Also included are interviews with the last remaining Sikh pilots from WWII, Air Chief Marshal Arjan Singh DFC and Mohinder Singh Pujji DFC, who are both now in their nineties.

Indian Air Force

Air Marshal Arjan Singh led pilots in the Burmese front in the Second World War and later led the Indo-Pak and Indo-China air assaults. Pujji had an impeccable record for bravery and saved a 300 strong Battalion of lost American soldiers that were given up for dead in the dense Burmese forests. Although the countless other Sikh pilots from the Great Wars are now deceased, their histories are represented by the recollections of outstanding pilots such as Manmohan Singh, Mehr Singh DSO, Prithpal Singh and Air Marshal Shivdev Singh.
This is the story of the Sikh pilots.

Cranwell

Royal Air Force Cranwell or more simply RAF Cranwell is a Royal Air Force station in Lincolnshire, England, close to the village of Cranwell, near Sleaford. Cranwell became the entry point for all those who wished to become permanent officers in the RAF, and the selection process was extremely stringent and initially the course took two years to train an officer.

Cranwell

Sardar Hardit Singh Malik
Commissioned in Royal Flying Corps in 1917
The very first Indian to fly, join the Royal Flying Corps, get his wings, go into aerial combat on the Western Front, shoot down German fighters and himself be seriously wounded in the air was an outstanding personality. Sardar, whose life and times were so extraordinary and his achievements so varied, that it is most meaningful to dwell upon his pioneering career. Born on 23RD November, 1892, to a distinguished Sikh family of Rawalpindi in the Punjab, Hardit Singh was educated at an English Public School (Eastbourne College), from where he went to Balliol College at Oxford. Graduating with honours, his scholastic achievements were matched by his sports prowess, getting his blues in cricket and golf. When the Great War broke out in 1914, he was in his second year at Oxford and practically all his British colleagues volunteered to join the fighting services.

Following a personal interview with General Henderson, Commanding the Royal Flying Corps, Hardit Singh joined the RFC as a cadet at Aldershot early in 1917, the first Indian, and Sikh, in any flying service in the world. A specially-designed flying helmet was worn by Hardit Singh over his turban. Hardit Singh was selected for fighters and went 'solo' in a Cauldron after just 2 1/2 hours instruction. Hardit Singh was posted to Filton, near Bristol, flying the Avro 504, the BE 2C, the Sopwith Pup, the Neiuport and finally the Sopwith Camel, the most advanced fighter at this time.

Cranwell

Sardar Hardit Singh Malik

At Filton, RFC pilots were taught combat tactics, including the famous Immelmann turn, Hardit Singh getting his wings in under a month. Posted to No.28 Squadron, equipped with the Camel, the formation soon flew out to St.Omer in France, then to an airfield in Flanders near the village of Droglandt. Here Lieutenant Hardit Singh Malik first met the new Commanding Officer, the legendary Major William G.Barkar who had come from Canada as a cavalryman in 1915, joined the RFC in 1916, and flew two seaters and fighters, becoming an ace many times over. Barkar was considered the greatest all-rounder pilot of World War One, and he personally initiated Hardit Singh into the art and science of aerial combat, leading him into the first actions including those against the legendary "Red Baron", Manfred von Richthofen's Staffel. In one major dog fight over 100 British and German fighters scrapping over the battle lines, Hardit Singh shot down his first German Fokker and was to go on to notch another eight aerial victories in the weeks ahead before he, himself, was wounded in action but survived in amazing circumstances. After months in hospital, Hardit Singh rejoined the service, now renamed as the Royal Air Force, flying the Bristol Fighter, probably the best fighter of the war, with No.141 Squadron at Biggin Hill, a specialist unit for defending London from raiding Zeppelins and Botha bombers.

Cranwell

Sardar Hardit Singh Malik

As described then, "One of the first to be posted to the new squadron was Lieutenant Hardit Singh Malik, a Sikh from Rawalpindi. A keen cricketer and golfer, Malik was one of the most popular officers at Biggin Hill. He staunchly refused to part with his turban and somehow managed to fit over it an outsized flying helmet, earning the affectionate nick name of "flying hobgoblin" from the ground crews.

Besides Malik the Sikh, the original fighter pilots of Biggin Hill included men from Australia, Canada, New Zealand, Rhodesia, Argentina, as well as the United Kingdom".

After the armistice, Hardit Singh was posted to another Brisfit Squadron, No.11, at Nivelles near Brussels before he finally returned home after the War, a hero in his own right. Hardit Singh Malik was to later join the prestigious Indian Civil Service. As a postscript, this remarkable man's chequered career included assignments as Trade Commissioner in London, Hamburg, Washington and Ottawa, becoming Prime Minister of Patiala State, later Indian High Commissioner to Canada, and Ambassador to France. After retirement in 1956, he returned to his first passion, golf becoming India's finest player ever, even with the two German bullets still embedded in his leg.

Hardit Singh Malik lived till he was 91, passing away in November 1985.

Cranwell

Bhupinder Singh and Amarjit Singh
Commissioned from Cranwell in 1932

In the competitive combined examination for admission to Cranwell in November 1929, was Bhupinder Singh, followed immediately by the highest-scoring candidate, his cousin, Amarjit Singh. These first Sikh cadets proceeded to England in September 1930. Amarjit Singh and Bhupinder Singh belonged to a well known Sikh family of Sargodha in the Punjab.

Amarjit studied at the Government College Lahore and Bhupinder at the Lahore Christian College. Both being great sportsmen at home, they were to make their mark in hockey and tennis while at Cranwell. After getting their "wings" in July 1932, they were the pioneers who formed "A" Flight of No. 1 Squadron of the Indian Air Force on 1ST April 1933. Tragically, both were killed in an air accident six months later during an air exercise near Hyderabad-Sind.

Pilot Officer Daljit Singh
Commissioned from Cranwell in 1933

Daljit Singh was sent to the Royal Air Force College at Cranwell and, after commissioning joined the No.1 Squadron Indian Air Force. However, Daljit Singh fell out with the Commanding Officer of the base and resigned his commission soon after.

Cranwell

Air Commodore Mehar Singh DSO, MVC,
Commissioned from Cranwell in 1938

Mehar Singh was selected for the Royal Indian Air Force in 1933 while he was in the final year of B.Sc. During his training at the Royal Air Force College at Cranwell in England, he impressed the college authorities by his single-mindedness, discipline and spirit of comradeship. This brave, yet unassuming and modest Air Officer won the admiration and affection of his seniors as also of the men under him. Asghar Khan, an Officer under him, who later became Chief of the Air Staff of Pakistan, said about him, "With the solitary exception of Squadron Leader Mehar Singh, a pilot of outstanding ability, no one was able to inspire confidence among us." After his training in England, Mehar Singh joined No 1 Squadron. In the operations in the wild and mountainous North West Frontier Province, he flew in one month as many as a hundred hours. He did the job so commendably that the next year he was called upon to evacuate refugees from Burma. In 1942, the Commander-in-Chief presented Mehar Singh a Commendation Certificate in recognition of his operational flying in Sind during the Hur disturbances in that province. A few months later, Mehar Singh accomplished a feat which, as per Air Officer Commanding-in-Chief, "any airman of any air force in the world would be proud to accomplish." Mehar Singh also took over the command of the Arakan area of Burma. There, too, he displayed his unique qualities of leadership and daring.

Cranwell

Air Commodore Mehar Singh DSO, MVC

Under the leadership of Mehar Singh Squadron No 6, with its Hurricanes, came to be known as the Eyes of the 14TH Army, commanded by Gen. William Slim. After the war, Field Marshall Slim recorded, "I was particularly impressed with the conduct of the Squadron led by a young Sikh Squadron Leader (Mehar Singh). They were a happy and efficient unit."

Remembering Mehar Singh, Lieutenant General Harwant Singh (Retd) observed, "Mehar Singh was one of the most celebrated fighter pilots of the Second World War. A pilot par excellence and a dare-devil, once in the cockpit, he became a part of the machinery." For his work in Arakan, which he accomplished with great skill and success, Mehar Singh was awarded DSO in March, 1944. In fact, he was the first and the only Officer of the IAF to have won this award. Mehar Singh, being fully adept at piloting Fighters, Bombers and Multi-engine Transport Planes, was asked to rescue women and children from a beleaguered Air Force station of Habbaniya in May, 1948. Soon after the war, Mehar Singh was called upon to assist in the task of reorganising and strengthening of the RIAF and the training of personnel. Promoted as Air Commodore in November, 1947, he took over Command No 1 Operational Group in Jammu and Kashmir. Mehar Singh was deeply attached to the Air Force, which made him an engineer and enabled him to gain experience in administration. He wished to leave it with honour but unfortunately that did not happen.

Cranwell

Air Commodore Mehar Singh DSO, MVC

In the interests of the Service, which he wanted to grow from strength to strength, he came to differ with some of his seniors on matters such as purchase of equipment, standard of discipline, programme for effectiveness, appointments, postings, and certain practices and trends in the administration.

Instead of getting involved in any controversy or confrontation that might have affected discipline in the Service, he chose to resign. He wished to be considered as one of those several hundreds of Airmen who had joined and served the RIAF and had been written off. At the same time, this Patriotic Air Fighter did not forget his obligation to his motherland. In the event of any emergency, he said, he would like to be the first to offer his services. Thus went away from the Indian Air Force a legendary hero on September 27TH 1948. When the Gallantry Awards were instituted, MVC (Maha Vir Chakra) was conferred upon Mehar Singh. An honour well deserved, indeed! But unfortunate as it may seem, it is, nevertheless, a fact that this nation soon forgets her sons who play heroic roles. What do we really do in this regard is a question to be pondered upon.

After his retirement, Mehar Singh was personal adviser of Maharaja Yadavindra Singh (of Patiala), the Rajparmukh of PEPSU. At times he would fly the Rajparmukh to New Delhi and other places for important conferences and meetings. He flew the Rajparmukh to New Delhi for the conference of Governors and Rajparmukh for the last time on March 11TH, 1952.

Cranwell

Air Commodore Mehar Singh DSO, MVC
He was to take the Maharaja back to Patiala on March 17TH. An aircraft of the Escorts Ltd. that he was flying from Jammu to New Delhi on the night of March 16TH was caught in a storm, killing Mehar Singh. A worthy life was thus cut short abruptly!

Maverick of the skies
By Lieutenant General Baljit Singh (Retd)

Once the history of any war is diligently imbibed, certain actions and deeds of individuals get imprinted so firmly in memory that they resurface time and again, with the least provocation. So it was that the mere mention of a school child's last name, a few days ago, brought to mind in a flash her late uncle, the indomitable Air Commodore Mehar Singh, D.S.O., M.V.C. Now, Squadron Leader Mehar Singh was conferred the first and the only D.S.O. of the Royal Indian Air Force during Second World War. Again, within weeks of India's Independence, Air Commodore Mehar Singh would be marked for the IAF's first Mahavir Chakra. On both occasions, recognition came for gallantry and exceptional leadership on the battlefield in two different wars and under gruelling circumstances. By the time Field Marshal William Slim launched the reinvigorated XIV Army to defeat the Japanese in the India-Burma theatre in 1944, Mehar Singh's actions and deeds had already placed him in the league of legends. His reputation was aptly and amusingly summed up by the Field Marshal in his memoirs, recounting an impromptu visit to No 6 Squadron of the RIAF in the Arakan (Burma):

Cranwell

Maverick of the skies

"The last air patrol had run into a bunch of Zeros (Japanese fighter aircraft) and had been shot down. The Sikh Squadron Leader, an old friend of mine, at once took out the next patrol himself and completed the mission. His methods, rumour had it, were a little unorthodox.

It was said that if any of his young officers made a bad landing, he would take them behind a *basha* and beat them. Whatever he did, it was effective; they were a happy, efficient and gallant squadron." It was not unusual to find entries in Mehar Singh's log book, flying upward of one hundred hours in a month, time and again. Flight Lieutenant Asghar Khan, who later became the Chief of Air Staff of Pakistan said: "With the solitary exception of Squadron Leader Mehar Singh, a pilot of exceptional ability, no one was able to inspire confidence among us." Mehar Singh was probably in the class of born ace pilots but more than that, he was innovative and daring in his modus operandi. It was an unmitigated tragedy when men of this one subcontinent would now be pitched in battles against each other, as citizens of two different nations. When on January 26TH, 1950, the Republic of India announced its first gallantry awards; Air Commodore Mehar Singh received the IAF's first Mahavir Chakra.

Unlike the foot soldiers, Mehar Singh in his fighter/bomber aircraft would be dropping bombs in the Poonch-Rajauri area in the west by night, and at dawn, strafing the enemy bunkers in the north along the Zojila La-Amaranth crest line, hundreds of kilometres apart.

Cranwell

Maverick of the skies

The moment of his ultimate glory came when he created aviation history by landing the first aircraft on the outskirts of Leh, by the banks of the river Indus. By January 1948, Pakistan's armed misadventure was fully contained in the Jammu region as also in the Srinagar valley.

But for Mehar Singh's innovative bombing with Dakotas, followed by the landing of the first one at a manually-levelled, mere 600-yard strip at Poonch, that tract of India would have been lost to Pakistan. However, it was the lack of road and aerial access to Ladakh year-long which was now a cause of serious concern. It was evident that for the moment airlift of troops and materials to Ladakh was the only course open. It was equally evident that the only man who could pioneer the aerial landing at Leh was Mehar Singh. In a one-to-one meeting, Major-Gen. K. S. Thimayya emphasized that "the fall of Leh would be a strategic blow to India. It had to be saved at all cost and that he was prepared to risk his own life with the IAF to save Leh." Mehar Baba (as the Air Commodore was now affectionately called) explained that "the Dakota was not designed to fly at such high attitude." General Thimayya knew that Mehar Singh never asked his subordinates to undertake a task that he himself had not first carried out, and so he closed the discussion on a positive note: "I will be on that flight in your cockpit. So let's go!" The stage was thus set for Mehar Baba when, on May 24TH, 1948, he landed the first Dakota at Leh, on an unprepared surface, 11,540 ft ASL.

Cranwell

Maverick of the skies

His passenger was Major-Gen. K. S. Thimayya D.S.O., GOC 19 Div. To land at Leh, one had to negotiate towering mountains in an ancient Dakota with no heating facilities, no pressurization and without any surveyed route map.

A great pity that no photo-record was made of the first landing, though the next flight of six Dakotas also led personally by Mehar Baba on May 28TH was fully covered. The aircraft and crews were literally engulfed this time by the astonished Ladakhis. Four months after the Leh landing, Mehar Singh resigned his commission. On March 11TH, 1952, nine days short of his 33RD birthday, he died when the Bonanza aircraft, caught in a freak, sudden storm crashed on the outskirts of Delhi, snuffing out a charmed life.

Cranwell

Squadron Leader Prithipal Singh
Commissioned from Cranwell in 1938
Sardar Prithipal Singh belonged to the Royal House of Patiala and completed his education at Atchison College Lahore, when he was selected for the Empire Pilot Training Course at RAF Cranwell in England. He was commissioned as Pilot Officer in the Indian Air Force on 23RD December 1939.

Flight Cadet Prithipal Singh, a tall, strikingly handsome Sikh from Aitcheson College, Lahore was one of the finest sportsmen at Cranwell, playing in the Cricket XI, Hockey XI and setting numerous records in athletics. His compatriot, Flight Cadet Arjan Singh, equally striking and well built, "played magnificently in the defence" in hockey for Cranwell and was awarded Blues in Athletics, Swimming and Hockey. Indian Flight Cadets who would, soon enough, prove their mettle in action during war operations, hardly three years from the time they left Cranwell.

The Indian Air Force had been formed on 8TH October 1932 with one squadron. No. 1 squadron and is the oldest squadron in the Indian Force. His first posting on being commissioned was flying Westland Wapiti biplanes in the North Western Frontier Province in support of the Indian Army operations against the insurgent tribesmen.

In 1939, the squadron was re-equipped with Hawker Hart aircraft with a few Hawker Audax aircraft on its inventory. In August 1941, the squadron was re-equipped with 12 Westland Lysander aircraft, financed as a gift from the citizens of Bombay.

Cranwell

Squadron Leader Prithipal Singh

In November 1941, the squadron moved en masse for an air display to Calcutta. When they returned they picked up a wrecked Lysander of No. 28 Squadron RAF and repaired it as their 13TH aircraft.

December 1941 saw the outbreak of the war in the Far East. Towards the end of December, it was known that the squadron would soon move to Burma to provide support in operations against the Japanese. The ground party left for Burma in the middle of January by train. The squadron with Flight Lieutenant Prithipal Singh flew its Lysanders across the country towards the end of January.

On 1ST February 1942 No.1 Squadron was moved to Taungoo in Burma to stem the Japanese offensive. The Lysanders were assigned to fly tactical reconnaissance missions. On the day of the induction, the area came under heavy air raids by the Japanese forces but due to effective dispersal, none of the aircraft were lost.

The retaliatory strikes were launched against the principal Japanese air bases at Mae-Haungsuan, Chiang Mai and Chiang Rai in Thailand. The missions were flown unescorted at low-level and the results were evident from the reduced air activity the following day. The Lysander was basically an army co-operation aircraft without a bomb sight. However, the squadron pilots perfected the techniques of dive bombing and carried out pin-point attacks. After a few days in Mingladon, Majumdar led one flight with Flight Lieutenant Prithipal Singh to Lashio to support the Chinese army operations.

Cranwell

Squadron Leader Prithipal Singh

Due to how well they performed, they were presented a "Gold Wing" by the Chinese. Throughout its span of operations, the squadron lost only one Lysander during operations, when the aircraft flipped over during a landing. At least one Lysander was lost in Japanese bombing and another lost during a ferry flight. One of the last missions was flown on 7TH March by Flying Officers Rajinder Singh and Raza. They flew two RAF pilots to Rangoon airfield to help evacuate two Hurricane fighters left behind at the airfield. The squadron handed over all but three of its Lysanders to the Burma Air Force that was newly raised.

The squadron had come back to Secunderabad in March 1942. On return from the fighting, the Squadron was converted to Hurricanes. After the conversion Prithipal Singh was promoted Squadron Leader and was given the command of the newly raised No. 3 Squadron. The Squadron was ordered to Burma and was tasked to carry out reconnaissance missions to gauge Japanese intentions. On the eve of their move to Burma the Squadron suffered an unfortunate loss; their Commanding Officer Squadron Leader Prithipal Singh failed to recover from a dive and crashed, instantly killing him.

It was a tragic loss to the fledgling Indian Air Force, for like his compatriot Arjan Singh, he was destined to be one of the leaders of the Indian Air Force.

Cranwell

Marshal of the Air Arjan Singh DFC, Padma Vibhushan
Commissioned from Cranwell in 1938

Marshal of the Indian Air Force Sardar Arjan Singh, DFC, was one Pilot who grew up in the annals of the Air Force as the first Chief for leading the force into war. He was Chief of Air Staff when the Indian Air Force saw action in its first combat in 1965. He was hardly 44 years of age when entrusted with the responsibility of leading the Indian Air Force. A responsibility he carried with considerable flamboyance and élan.

Arjan Singh was born on 15TH April 1919, in Lyallpur, completing his education at Montgomery. He was 19 years of age when he was selected for the Empire Pilot Training Course at RAF at Cranwell. His first posting on being commissioned was flying Westland Wapiti biplanes in the North Western Frontier Province. Arjan Singh flew against the tribal forces, before he was transferred for a brief stint with the newly formed No.2 IAF Squadron. Later he moved back to No.1 as a Flying Officer, when the Squadron re-equipped with the Hawker Hurricane. Promoted to Squadron Leader in 1944, Arjan Singh led the Squadron against the Japanese during the Arakan Campaign. Flying close support during the crucial Imphal Campaign and later assisting the advance of the Allied Forces to Rangoon, Burma. For his role in successfully leading the Squadron in combat, Arjan Singh received the Distinguished Flying Cross (DFC) in 1944. He was given command of the IAF Display Flight, flying Hawker Hurricanes after the war, which toured India giving demonstrations.

Cranwell

Marshal of the Air Arjan Singh

On 15TH August 1947, he had the unique honour of leading the fly-past of over a hundred IAF aircraft over the red fort in Delhi. Promoted to Wing Commander, he attended Staff College in UK, and immediately after Indian Independence became the AOC, Ambala in the rank of Group Captain. In 1949, promoted to Air Commodore, Arjan Singh took over the Air Officer Commanding of Operational Command, which later came to be known as Western Air Command. Arjan Singh had the distinction of having the longest tenure as the AOC of Operational Command, from 1949-1952 and again from 1957-1961. Promoted to Air Vice Marshal, he was the AOC-in-C of Operational Command.

Towards the end of the 1962 war, he was appointed the DCAS and became the VCAS by 1963. He was the overall Commander of the joint air training exercises "Shiksha" held between the IAF, RAF and RAAF.

On 1ST August 1964, Arjan Singh took over as the Chief of Air Staff in the rank of Air Marshal, which became the pinnacle of this career. Having flown over 60 different types of aircraft from Pre-WW-2 era biplanes to the more contemporary, Gnats & Vampires, he also had flown in transports like the Super Constellation. Arjan Singh's testing time came in September 1965, when the subcontinent was plunged into war. When Pakistan launched its Operation Grand Slam, in which an armoured thrust targeted the vital town of Akhnur, he was summoned into the Defence Minister's office with a request for air support.

Cranwell

Marshal of the Air Arjan Singh
With a characteristic non-chalance, he replied "...in an hour." And true enough, the Air Force struck the Pakistani offensive in an hour. It must be said that the credit for thwarting Ayub Khan's grandiose plans to capture Kashmir is shared by the Indian Army and the Indian Air Force, and Arjan Singh for leading the Air Force through the war. Arjan Singh was awarded the Padma Vibhushan for his leadership of the Air Force, and subsequently in recognition of the Air Force's contribution in the war, the rank of the CAS was upgraded to that of Air Chief Marshal and Arjan Singh became the first Air Chief Marshal of the Indian Air Force. He retired in August 1969, thereupon accepting ambassadorship to Switzerland.

He remained a flyer to the end of his tenure in the IAF, visiting forward Squadrons & Units and flying with them. Arjan Singh was a source of inspiration to a generation of Indians and Officers. In recognition of his Services, the Government of India conferred the rank of Marshal of the Air Force onto Arjan Singh in January 2002 making him the first and the only 'Five Star' rank Officer with the Indian Air Force.

In honour of his service, on 14TH April 2016 at an event to mark the Marshal's 97TH birthday, Chief of Air Staff Air Chief Marshal Arup Raha announced that the Indian Air Force base at Panagarh in West Bengal was to be named after MIAF Arjan Singh and to be called Air Force Station Arjan Singh from then on.

Kenya

In 1888, the Imperial British East Africa Company (I.B.E.A.C.) took over the British concessions negotiated with the Sultan of Zanzibar, which also included Kenya. In the early stages of British occupation, I.B.E.A.C set up a police force, primarily to buttress the occupying power. This force drew armed African guards - known as Askaris - into its rank and file under the command of Somali and Sikh officers, with a few Europeans filling its uppermost echelons. By 1897, the I.B.E.A.C had set up a police headquarters in Mombasa and command stations in Vangu, Rabai, Malindi, Lamu, and Kismayu. By 1902, police units had been set up in Nairobi, Mombasa, and Kisumu. These units were soon brought under a single command named the British East Africa Police that would later, in 1920 with the emergence of Kenya Colony, be renamed the Kenya Police. The British are known as great organisers and in view of that a proper police force was established with the help of Indians from India, especially the Sikhs, who were well known for their valour and loyalty.

These sturdy men, who were skilled and semi skilled artisans, were a great help in building the country. The British were aware of the faithfulness and the bravery of the Sikhs, thereby giving them the jobs, which were suitable to their character. The skilled and semi skilled labour force was one aspect and the administration side the other, where the more educated ones were employed to do the clerical work of the East African railways. The Police force grew from strength to strength with plenty of Sikhs serving diligently and reaching top posts.

Kenya

The authorities in Kenya also encouraged the Sikh farmers of the Punjab into a settlement perched above the shores of Lake Victoria at Kibos. The Kibos settlement originated with the award of small plots of land, in a swampy area six miles from the Lake. The settlement soon spread and was planted with cotton, rice, wheat, sugar cane, and other crops. Beyond the land itself, the government provided other inducements for the Sikhs to settle in Kenya.

The Sikhs had become so entrenched into Kenya that even when Kenya became a sovereign state, the Sikhs retained their employment in the military and police forces, in which they attained very high ranks. In fact the Sikhs became a distinct tribe in Kenya. This is the story of just one of the Sikhs, Lieutenant Colonel Gurcharan Singh Chana, who attended Cranwell Academy in the United Kingdom.

Lieutenant Colonel Gurcharan Singh Chana,
Trained at Cranwell

Lieutenant Colonel Gurcharan Singh Chana was born in a poor family. Whilst in school it was his desire to become a Pilot. After finishing his education he briefly worked for a bank and at the same time acquired a Private Pilot's License. He then decided to join the Kenya Air Force. He completed his Officer Training with the Royal Air Force at Cranwell in England and on his return he was commissioned into Kenya Armed Forces by the Late President His Excellency Mzee Jomo Kenyatta.

Kenya

Lieutenant Colonel Gurcharan Singh Chana,
As he progressed in the Air Force, as a Pilot, he was the first Sikh to be awarded the rank of a Lieutenant Colonel. Subsequently he was the first Kenyan Sikh to acquire the position of Station Commander Kenya Air Force. After serving for 20 years in the Air Force, he retired in 1985. He then joined Kenya Airways as a Pilot and having flown most of the aircraft in Kenya Airways he retired as a Captain and Boeing Instructor. He has flown a total of 15 different types of aeroplanes. He also had a deep passion to go into music and he learned Tabla at the age of 6 years from the great Gurus in India. He practiced regularly and today is regarded as the top percussionist on the Tabla in Africa. He has accompanied the great King of Ghazals Jagjit Singh, Sitar Maestro Ustad Basharat Khan, Ustad Mehdi Hassan and Parvez Mehndi. In addition he has also given numerous musical performances with most of the leading professional artists in the World. Channi, as he is more prominently known, was very close to Jagjit Singh. One of his great moments was when Jagjit Ji came to Nairobi and invited Channi to perform with him on the stage. Channi is married to his charming wife Jaswant Kaur (Jassy). They have two daughters namely Taninder and Maninder and a son Ishwinder, all Southampton University Graduates.

Brigadier Surjit Singh Plaha
Surjit Singh attained the rank of Brigadier in the Kenya Army. (The author has been unable to find the bio data of the good Brigadier).

Royal Air Force

Air Vice Marshal Harjinder Singh MBE, PVSM
Commissioned in the IAF in 1931

Harjinder Singh was born on 4TH February, 1909. Having joined the Indian Air Force as a Hawai Sepoy (Air Soldier), a rank lower than that of a Soldier, Harjinder Singh rose to become an Air Vice Marshal. He dominated the technical side of the Indian Air Force's earlier years and made the Indian Air Force the only Air Force in the world to undertake manufacture of aircraft.

The key to an effective fighting air arm would not only be the aviators but aircraft, men, mechanics and technical tradesmen who would constitute its backbone. To the good fortune of the future Indian Air Force, amongst the first to apply were a number of well educated, highly motivated and patriotic individuals who sacrificed better emoluments in order to join what they felt was an important contribution to a future free India. One of them was Harjinder Singh, then studying at the Maclaghen Engineering College, Lahore but for some time obsessed with joining the Air Force. He was amongst the first nine Engineering Students to be selected in November 1930. He joined the 1ST Squadron, Indian Air Force, in January, 1931, at Karachi. In the years 1933 to 1937 the Squadron trained for its primary role of Army Co-operation from Drigh Road, Peshawar, Chaklala and Sialkot. As a Non Commissioned Officer, Harjinder Singh saw extensive service in continuous operations against hostile tribesmen in the North West Frontier Province.

Royal Air Force

Air Vice Marshal Harjinder Singh MBE, PVSM
On 3RD September, 1939, Harjinder Singh was offered a commission in the Royal Air Force, so he could command 500 Indian non-Combatant Section personnel working for the Royal Air Force. He declined the offer. 'I felt too strongly the esprit de corps of our fledgling Service to desert them for the sake of a Commission'. On 1ST November, Harjinder Singh was promoted to the rank of Sergeant (Hawai Havildar). In November 1941, the Squadron moved en masse for an air display to Calcutta. On their return, when they had touched down at Lahore to refuel, Harjinder saw a damaged Lysander of No. 28 Squadron RAF classified as Category 'E'; that is beyond repair. 'I told Majumdar (Squadron Leader) that I would go on ahead to Lahore and repair the crashed Lysander: then when our Squadron passed through Lahore, it could pick up the aircraft as a moral claim and just annexe to our Squadron!' Harjinder picked up the wrecked Lysander and repaired it as their 13TH aircraft!

December 1941 saw the outbreak of the war in the Far East. On 1ST February 1942, No. 1 Squadron moved to Taungoo, Burma. Warrant Officer Harjinder Singh, who had improvised a wooden tail wheel for the Lysanders when the spares ran out, was appointed Member of the Order of the British Empire for his imaginative improvisation and for maintaining very high aircraft serviceability in spite of poor logistic backing. Harinder Singh was commissioned as Flying Officer in the Indian Air Force on 3RD September 1942 and rose to become Air Vice Marshal.

Royal Air Force

Air Vice Marshal Harjinder Singh MBE, PVSM

He was an engineering genius who had a vision ahead of his time. His vision to produce the first transport aircraft within the country led to IAF, Indian Airlines and a few other operators using aircraft made indigenously. This is a fantastic legacy we owe to Air Vice Marshal Harjinder Singh's drive and dedication. Maintenance Command was formed at Kanpur on 26TH January 1955, with Air Vice Marshal Harjinder Singh as its first Air Officer Commander-in-Chief. Kanpur was the core centre of maintenance activities even before Independence. A unit called Aircraft Manufacturing Depot was subsequently added to undertake manufacture of AVRO aircraft. As Kanpur alone was not able to absorb the futuristic industrial activities, Nagpur was eventually selected as the new site for setting up Maintenance Command Headquarters. Maintenance Command was set up to provide maintenance support to operating bases both by undertaking service and repair of aircraft, aero engines, ground equipments, radars and missiles and warehousing of stores required during peace and war. These works are undertaken by Base Repair Depots, Equipment Depots and Air Storage Parks. These units have the most modern and state of the art equipment to undertake repair and service of various weapon systems.

Harjinder Singh retired as AOC-in-C of the Maintenance Command in 1964.

Air vice Marshal Harjinder Singh passed away in November 1971. An entire colony in Kanpur has been named as Harjinder Nagar after him.

Royal Air Force

Flying Officer Man Mohan Singh
Commissioned in the IAF in 1939
Man Mohan Singh son of Dr. Makhan Singh was born in Rawalpindi, now in Pakistan, in September 1906. Dr Makhan Singh was a recipient of the Kaisar-i-Hind medal from the government for his distinguished public service as a medical practitioner.

Man Mohan Singh was educated at Denny's High School and at Gordon College, both in Rawalpindi. In 1923, at the age of 17 he went to England to train as a civil engineer, receiving his B.Sc degree four years later at the University of Bristol. Flying Officer Man Mohan Singh
In England he also completed a two-year course in flying and aeronautical engineering for which he had been given a scholarship by the Government of British India. Man Mohan Singh therefore became one of the very first Sikh aviators.

Competing for the Aga Khan prize of 500 pounds Man Mohan Singh made two attempts during January-February 1930 in completing a solo flight between England and India. His first flight was on 24TH January 1930 when he took off from Croydon near London in a single-engine light aircraft, reaching Rome on 30TH January. From Rome he flew to Naples, but was thereafter forced to land in thick fog on a mountain road in southern Italy. His machine was badly damaged and Man Mohan Singh also suffered injury on the left eye. His second attempt too had to be abandoned midway.

Royal Air Force

Flying Officer Man Mohan Singh

Taking off from Karachi on 3RD March 1930, another competitor for the prize, R.N. Chawla, succeeded in reaching England in 17 days, however he was not considered eligible for the prize, for he had carried with him a companion, A.M. Engineer, another pilot.

This gave Manmohan Singh his third chance. He took off from Croydon on 8TH April 1930 and reached Karachi, but not within the stipulated period of one month, losing time owing to a forced landing he had to make in a swamp at St. Rambert, near Marseilles (southern France). The Aga Khan prize went to A.M. Engineer, who taking off from England on 25TH April 1930 reached Karachi on 11TH May. Another competitor for the Aga Khan prize on this occasion was J.R.D. Tata who later became famous as a businessman. Man Mohan Singh missed the prize, but he was the first Sikh and Indian to complete a solo flight from England to India.

Appreciating his perseverance, Maharaja Bhupinder Singh, ruler of Patiala state, compensated him for the lost prize and gave him employment as his chief pilot. In 1934-35, Manmohan Singh became the first Sikh and Indian to successfully complete a solo journey from England to South Africa in a light aircraft.

At the outbreak of World War II in 1939, Man Mohan Singh joined the Indian Air Force Volunteer Reserve as a pilot officer. He was selected leader of an Indian Air Force batch of pilots sent to England for training and active duty.

Royal Air Force

As the oldest of the group he was affectionately known as *Chacha* (Punjabi for Uncle)

While in England he was known to have a cold shower every morning and not to eat anything until he had recited the Sikh prayer of *Japji Sahib* (one of the Sikh morning prayers). Air Marshall Shivdev Singh, one of the group of Indian pilots that trained in England with Man Mohan Singh once was quoted as attributing his fame, "to mistaken identity, that with Chacha Man Mohan Singh".

Given Man Mohan Singh's long and varied flying experience, he was given immediate command of a Sunderland flying boat with the RAF Coastal Command, hunting submarines during the battle for the Atlantic. Man Mohan Singh was later promoted to flying officer in the British Indian Air Force and given the command of a Catalina aircraft in the No. 205 squadron for operations in the Philippines and Indonesia. Having suffered heavy losses during operations to locate the Japanese invasion fleets, No. 205 squadron withdrew from Singapore and relocated to Java. When the Japanese forces invaded Java the squadron retired to Australia.

On 3RD March 1942, Japanese air attack consisting of nine Mitsubishi Zeros destroyed all fifteen flying boats still on the water in Broome harbour. 88 people were killed. Man Mohan Singh was in a Catalina at the time the attack occurred. He is thought to have survived the shelling and resulting explosion however as Man Mohan Singh could not swim he drowned in the ocean. A truly forgotten hero!

Royal Air Force

Air Marshal Shivdev Singh,
Commissioned in the IAF 1940

Air Marshal Shivdev Singh was the last of the survivors of the batch of 24 Indian Air Force Fighter Pilots who were seconded to the Royal Air Force, as part of the reinforcement the British desperately needed in 1940 to fight the "Battle of Britain". Flying Sterlings over occupied France and Germany - including daring attacks on their submarine pens - he was decorated for Gallantry in a campaign that had many casualties. He was rushed back home when the Japanese conquered Burma and flew the Hurricanes in the Arakan within Burma. One of the pioneers of the Indian Air Force, Shivdev Singh, was responsible for the evacuation of his Squadron from Kohat to Chaklala at the time of Partition in 1947. He later moved to Agra to found the Transport Squadron. Besides flying the political leaders of the day, Shivdev and his men organized the massive airlift to Srinagar in time to save the Kashmir Valley from Pakistani raiders. What makes his contribution to the IAF unique is that he was perhaps the most operationally experienced Commander. He was in charge of the IAF's role in "Operation Vijay" in the liberation of Goa. The IAF Fighter Pilots played no major role in the 1962 Sino-Indian conflict. But the subsequent training for Air Defence Operations named "Operation Shiksha" again had Shivdev Singh in command. The crowning glory was his role as the Vice-Chief, when he master-minded the entire Air Operations in the 1971 Indo-Pak war.

Royal Air Force

Air Marshal Shivdev Singh,
Although the Chief, P.C. Lal, was given the credit publically, the man at the head of the operation table was Shivdev Singh. The story going on in the IAF circles is that Shivdev Singh almost made it to the top job as Lal's successor. The then Defence Minister, Jagjivan Ram was even supposed to have telephoned him saying, "Let me be the first to congratulate you" - after the appointment had been cleared at the highest level. But things changed overnight for reasons well beyond the reach of the high-flying IAF brass - as often happens in a corrupt India. Shivdev Singh retired - but without any rancour - to his home in Chandigarh, contributing gracefully to Public Service in the Punjab.

Air Marshal Shivdev Singh passed away in January, 1994,

Squadron Leader Mohinder Singh Pujji, DFC, PCS, BA, LLB
Commissioned in the IAF 1940
Mohinder Singh Pujji was born in Simla, British India, on 14TH August 1918, the fourth son of Sardar Sohan Singh Pujji and Sant Kaur. His father was a senior government official who worked in the Department of Health and Education. He attended the Sir Harcourt Butler High School in Simla, and then on his father's retirement to his home state of Punjab attended the Government College and later the Hindu College in Lahore.

He learned to fly in 1936 at the Delhi Flying Club, where he fell in love with flying and in April 1937 received his Indian commercial 'A' pilot's licence.

Royal Air Force

Squadron Leader Mohinder Singh Pujji

His first job was as a pilot with Himalayan Airways, flying passengers between Hardwar and Badrinath, but soon after was offered a better job with Burmah Shell as a refuelling superintendent in 1938.

In 1940, he attended the Indian Air Force 4TH Pilots Course, and became one of the first batch of 24 Indian 'A' licence holder pilots accepted to receive a Volunteer Reserve commission with the Royal Air Force during the early part of the Second World War, despite his parents' fears.

Embarking for the United Kingdom, his first posting was on 8TH October 1940 to No. 1 RAF Depot in Uxbridge. Within a few days he was posted to No. 12 Elementary Flying Training School RAF at Prestwick in Scotland. From there the first 24 volunteer Indian pilots went on to No. 9 (Pilot) Advanced Flying Unit RAF at RAF Hullavington. They completed the course and received their RAF wings on 16TH April 1941. A few weeks later he and a handful of other pilots from the first 24 went on to the renowned No. 56 Operational Training Unit (OTU) at RAF Sutton Bridge, where they joined British and other foreign-allied pilots for advanced fighter pilot training on the Hawker Hurricane.

Officially he flew active service just after the Battle of Britain, joining No. 43 Squadron RAF, the formidable 'Fighting Cocks' fighter squadron. He flew Hurricanes, which he preferred to Spitfires, for their relative ease of flying.

Royal Air Force

Squadron Leader Mohinder Singh Pujji

He was forced down twice; in one instance, his aircraft was disabled over the English Channel by a Messerschmitt, but he managed to coax it to dry land, where he crashed. He was rescued from the burning wreckage and after a week in hospital, Mohinder Singh returned to duty.

He was treated well in England, getting preferential treatment at local cinemas and restaurants, often without payment.

He subsequently commented, "I felt very welcome indeed, I never felt different or an outsider and my experiences in this country made me keen to return some time after the war. I was made to feel very much at home by everyone I met" and "I wrote back to my father saying that I did not mind if I was killed because the British people were wonderful and so brave, and I was being so well treated. I could not queue for a movie without being told to move to the front." As a Sikh, he insisted on retaining his dastar (Sikh headdress), with RAF insignia, even while flying, even carrying a spare, in case it was needed. The dastar interfered with use of his oxygen mask and resulted in damage to his lungs.

After the Battle of Britain, Mohinder Singh was sent to the Middle East where, in 1941, he was forced down, for the second time, in the North African desert and was picked up by British troops. He had dietary problems, as he could not eat the standard issue bully beef for religious reasons.

Royal Air Force

Squadron Leader Mohinder Singh Pujji
He returned to south Asia and served in Afghanistan and Burma, where he was awarded the DFC.[1][6] Announced in The London Gazette on 17TH April 1945, and followed with a personal letter of congratulations from Air Chief Marshal Sir Keith Park, the DFC citation reads in part:

Acting Flight Lieutenant Mohinder Singh Pujji No. 4 (RIAF) Squadron

> "This officer has flown on many reconnaissance sorties over Japanese occupied territory, often in adverse monsoon weather. He has obtained much valuable information on enemy troop movements and dispositions, which enabled an air offensive to be maintained against the Japanese troops throughout the monsoon. Flight Lieutenant Pujji has shown himself to be a skilful and determined pilot who has always displayed outstanding leadership and courage."

In late 1946, after suffering from a long illness of tuberculosis, which nearly cost him his life; caused him to become classified unfit for military service and receive a permanent disability discharge from the Royal Indian Air Force. From 1947, Mohinder Singh was employed as an Aerodrome Officer at Safdarjung Aerodrome Delhi, where he also continued to fly in a civilian role. He went on to aspire as a champion air race pilot and holder of gliding records. Mohinder Singh moved to East Ham, England, after retirement and he became an active member of the local community. Later, he settled in Gravesend, Kent.

Royal Air Force

Squadron Leader Mohinder Singh Pujji
On 12TH October 2000, he was made an Honorary Freeman of the Borough of Newham.

In 2005, Mohinder Singh protested against the British National Party's use of an image of a Spitfire in their campaign literature. He was reported as saying,
"The BNP are wrong to use the Spitfire as representative of their party. They forget people from different backgrounds helped in the Second World War. I am proof of this - I was flying a Spitfire. I also met Winston Churchill. Even in those days, there were ethnic minorities fighting for the British. I would recommend the armed forces for young people, regardless of race." In August 2010, his autobiography *For King And Another Country* was released.

Mohinder Singh Pujji died of a stroke at Darent Valley Hospital on 18TH September 2010, aged 92. The local authority Gravesham Borough Council, celebrated his life and heroism with an exhibition.

In 2011 the short film The Volunteers was dedicated to Mohinder after he contributed to the making, but died before the films completion.

Despite the high respect that he experienced during the war, Mohinder Singh believed that war films presented a "white-only view of the RAF". He campaigned to have the Sikh contribution to the British war effort, which he believed had been ignored, more widely recognised. He was never invited to any of the many events in Britain that marked the 70TH anniversary of the outbreak of World War II in 2010, or any other year, he says.

Royal Air Force

Squadron Leader Mohinder Singh Pujji

He is quoted as saying, "As far as I think, no one in authority remembers that we are here and we were a part of World War II".

In an effort to redress the balance, the Royal Air Force Museum Cosford opened a permanent exhibition in January 2009 ("Diversity in the Royal Air Force"), intended to "challenge negative perceptions, by celebrating the racial diversity of its history". Mohinder Singh was the guest of honour at the opening.

A statue of Squadron Leader Pujji by Douglas Jennings was unveiled in St. Andrew's Gardens, Gravesend on 28TH November 2014. It bears the inscription: "To commemorate those from around the world who served alongside Britain in all conflicts 1914-2014".

Indian Navy

With Vice Admiral Harinder Singh (Retd) Indian Navy

India has a rich maritime heritage. There is also plenty of evidence derived from Indian literature and art, including sculpture and painting, besides the evidence of archaeology to suggest the antiquity of the Indian maritime tradition. The origin of the Indian Navy goes back to the English East India Company which set up the force and named it the Honourable East India Company's Marine, after they encountered and defeated the Portuguese at the Battle of Swally off Diu. The first fighting ships arrived on 5TH September 1612. This force protected merchant shipping off the Gulf of Cambay and the rivers Tapti and Narmada.

In 1686, with most of English commerce moving to Bombay, the force was renamed the Bombay Marine. The Bombay Marine was involved in combat against the Marathas and the Sidis and participated in the Anglo-Burmese Wars. The Bombay Marine recruited many Indian lascars but commissioned no Indian Officers until 1928. In 1830, the Bombay Marine became Her Majesty's Indian Navy. The British capture of Aden increased the commitments of Her Majesty's Indian Navy, leading to the creation of the Indus Flotilla. The Navy then fought in the China War of 1840. Her Majesty's Indian Navy resumed the name Bombay Marine from 1863 to 1877, when it became Her Majesty's Indian Marine. The Marine then had two Divisions; the Eastern Division at Calcutta and the Western Division at Bombay. In recognition of the services rendered during various campaigns, Her Majesty's Indian Marine was titled the Royal Indian Marine in 1892 (RIM). By this time it consisted of over 50 vessels.

Indian Navy

The Royal Indian Marine did not make any significant contribution to the maritime history of India from 1892 till the outbreak of World War One. Before the war, the main task assigned to the RIM was maritime survey, maintainace of light houses and transportation of troops. During the war, there were notable exploits of the RIM in various theatres of naval operations. Its ships transported troops, arms, ammunition and stores to Egypt, Iraq and East Africa. While on patrol in the Suez Canal, the *RIM Hardinge* fought against the Turks and thwarted their efforts to block the canal. During the action she suffered severe damage and lost one of her funnels but succeeding in preventing the blocking of the canal. RIM ships landed troops in Mesopotamia and its smaller ships, designed for operations in inland waters, rendered excellent service in the Euphrates, Tigres, the Euphrates and Shatt-al-Arab, in order to keep the supply lines open for the troops fighting in Mesopotamia. A hospital ship operated by the Indian Marine was deployed to treat wounded soldiers. Three other ships, the *Northbrook*, *Minto* and *Dufferin* carried out patrolling in the Red Sea. While carrying these duties, the *Minto* called at Jeddah and transported some Haj Pilgrims safely back to India. By the time the war ended in 1918, the Royal Indian Marine suffered 330 casualties and 80 of its personnel were decorated with gallantry awards for service in the war. The Royal Indian Marine played a vital role in supporting and transporting the Indian Army throughout the war. The RIM was once again reverted to its no combatant role in 1918 after the end of the war.

Indian Navy

At the end of the war the task of naval defence of India once again entrusted to the Royal Navy, the combatant status of the RIM had been lost. The RIM was reconstituted as a combatant force in 1928 and the White Ensign was hoisted for the first time in its history on November 11TH, 1928. On October 2^{ND,} 1934, the Royal Indian Navy (RIN) came into being with the Naval Headquarters at Bombay under the Flag Officer Commanding Indian Navy.

At the start of the Second World War, the RIN undertook the task building, commissioning and working up fast seagoing motor boats for coastal patrol and corvettes and minesweepers which were suitably armed and equipped for carrying out anti-submarine and escort duties in the waters around India. The first Basset class trawler, *HMIS Travancore,* was built at Calcutta and commissioned into the RIN in July 1941. This was followed by five more within a year and another six soon thereafter. The first Bangor class minesweeper was built in India joined the RIN in 1943. To reinforce the RIN fleet, six sloops built in Great Britain and named after the Indian rivers, the *Jumna, Sutlej, Cauvery, Kistna, Godavari* and *Narbada* were also acquired soon.

Sloops of the RIN took part in operations in the Red Sea, Gulf of Aden and the Persian Gulf in 1940. The *Jumna* and *Sutlej* took part in the Battle of Atlantic in 1941. In the same year, reoccupation of Berbera in the Gulf of Aden was made possible by the first combined operations, i.e. amphibious operations, by the Indian Army and the Royal Indian Navy.

Indian Navy

The RIN also played a vital role during the advance of the Allied forces in Sudan. While *HMIS Clive* softened up the area between Port Sudan and Massawa with her armament and *HMIS Hindustan, Indus, Parvati* and *Ratnagiri* led the attack, the port of Massawa was taken from the Italians.

HMIS Bengal, a Bathurst class minesweeper of the RIN, covered herself in glory on November 11TH, 1942, while escorting a Dutch tanker, *HMIS Odina*, from Freemantle in Australia to Diego Garcia; she was attacked by two Japanese 10,000 ton armed merchant raiders. The raiders opened fire, but the *Bengal* could defend herself with one 12 pounder gun and few close-range anti-aircraft guns. Instead of making an attempt to escape, the *Bengal* instructed the *Odina* to increase her distance from the raiders and she pressed home an attack. The raiders opened fire once again at 3,500 yards and the *Bengal* retaliated with her small calibre armament. Her first salvo hit one of the raiders fortuitously landed on the latter's magazine resulting in an inferno which caused the raider to blow and sink within minutes. The second raider soon left the scene after causing considerable damage to the *Odina* and killing few members of her crew including the Commanding Officer. Though the *Bengal* suffered damage in the superstructure, no lives had been lost and the minesweeper was still operational. The *Odina* was virtually immobilised but the *Bengal*, succeeding in escorting her back to Freemantle.

Indian Navy

Ships of the RIN carried out sustained attacks on the Arakan Coast of Burma while operating from Chittagong and Koronge Island. They also provided close support to troops that had been landed by the RIN landing craft for driving the Japanese away from the area. Despite its success in operations in various theatres of war around the globe, the losses suffered by the RIN were negligible and the ships of the RIN and there men were still 'raring to go' when VJ Day arrived.

A victory parade was held in London on June 8TH, 1946 in which represented of the three Indian Armed Forces participate. The Naval Contingent was led by Lieutenant (later Rear Admiral) P.S. Mahindroo. In keeping with the inter-service seniority in which the Navy was the senior service, the parade was led by the Naval Contingent.

In 1947, British India was partitioned and the Union of India and Dominion of Pakistan gained independence from the United Kingdom. The Royal Indian Navy was split between India and Pakistan, with senior British officers continuing to serve with both navies, and the vessels were divided between the two nations.

The officer corps of the Indian Navy in the years after Independence was organised in four main branches viz, Executive, Engineering, Electrical and Supply and Secretarial. The Executive branch is the main operations branch and has four main specialisations viz Torpedo and Anti-Submarine warfare, Gunnery, Navigation and Direction and the Communication Branches. The role of the other branches is self-explanatory.

Indian Navy

Officers who served on board submarines or in Aviation also had the same specialisations. Only, officers of the Executive Branch can Command ships or are the second in Command. Similarly in the senior ranks, only Executive Officers can command the Fleet, be the Commander in Chief of a Command or be the Chief of the Naval Staff.

The first involvement of the Indian Navy in any conflict came during the 1961 Indian annexation of Goa with the success of Operation Vijay against the Portuguese Navy. Four Portuguese frigates - the *NRP Afonso de Albuquerque, the NRP Bartolommeo Dias, the NRP João de Lisboan* and the *NRP Gonçalves Zarco* - were deployed to patrol the waters off Goa, Daman and Diu, along with several patrol boats (Lancha de Fiscalização).

Eventually only the *NRP Afonso de Albuquerque* saw action against Indian Navy ships, the other ships having fled before commencement of hostilities. The *NRP Afonso* was destroyed by Indian frigates *INS Betwa* and *INS Beas*. Parts of the *Afonso* are on display at the Naval Museum in Mumbai, while the remainder was sold as scrap.

The Indian Navy played a significant role in the bombing of Karachi harbour in the 1971 war. On 4TH December, it launched Operation Trident during which missile boats *INS Nirghat* and *INS Nipat* sunk the minesweeper *PNS Muhafiz* and destroyer *PNS Khyber*. The destroyer *PNS Shahjahan* was irreparably damaged. Owing to its success, 4TH December has been celebrated as Navy Day ever since.

Indian Navy

The operation was so successful that the Pakistani Navy raised a false alarm about sighting an Indian missile boat on 6TH December. Pakistan Air Force (PAF) planes attacked the supposed Indian ship and damaged the vessel before it was identified as being another Pakistani Navy ship, *PNS Zulfiqar* which suffered numerous casualties and damage as a result of this friendly fire.

During Operation Python on 8TH December, the frigate *PNS Dacca* was severely damaged by *INS Veer* and the oil storage depot of Karachi was set ablaze. On the western front in the Arabian Sea, operations ceased after the Karachi port became unusable due to the sinking of Panama vessel *Gulf Star*. An Indian frigate, *INS Khukri* was sunk by submarine *PNS Hangor*.

On the eastern front, the submarine *PNS Ghazi* was sunk outside Vishakhapatnam harbour. Indian naval aircraft, Sea Hawks and Alizés, from the aircraft carrier *INS Vikrant* were instrumental in sinking many gunboats and merchant navy vessels in the Bay of Bengal. The successful blockade of East Pakistan by the Indian Navy proved to be a vital factor in the Pakistani surrender.

During the 2006, Lebanon War, the Indian Navy launched Operation Sukoon to successfully evacuate 2280 persons from Lebanon, including Indian, 436 Sri Lankan and 69 Nepali and 7 Lebanese citizens. Since 2ND November 2008 an Indian Navy frigate *INS Tabar* accompanied by the destroyer *INS Mysore* has been on an anti-piracy mission off the Gulf of Aden.

Indian Navy

Rear Admiral Pritam Singh Mahindroo
Commissioned in Indian Navy in 1939

Sardar Pritam Singh Mahindroo took to sea at the age of 16, as a sailor in the merchant navy. Six years later, he left the merchant navy and joined the Indian Navy immediately after Second World War started. Initially he was denied entry because, being a Sikh, he refused to cut his hair. In 1939, he joined with his turban on.

Between 1943 and 1944, he was the only Indian among 14 British officers on Indian Naval Ship (INS) *Godavari*. Mahindroo represented the Navy at the Victory Parade in London in 1945.

Mahindroo reminisces on the occasion, "Needless to say, that as turbaned officer leading the Naval Contingent, I was most prominent and I must have given hundreds of autographs amongst thousands of spectators who probably slept on the pavement for one or two nights to witness this historic parade."

Following Independence, he became the second-in-command of the destroyer *INS Rajput* and, in 1953, was appointed chief instructor at Staff College, Wellington. In 1961 Indian Navy had purchased the British aircraft carrier, *HMS Hercules* which was renamed *INS Vikrant* and Pritam Singh Mahindroo was chosen to pilot the ship from Belfast to Bombay. And so it was that *INS Vikrant* - steamed into the Arabian Sea in November 1961, with Mahindroo at the helm. A position he was to retain for the next three years as the 16,000 tonne aircraft carrier became a familiar symbol of India's growing defence capability.

Indian Navy

Rear Admiral Pritam Singh Mahindroo
To his eternal regret, Mahindroo was never given the command of a fleet or the honour to fly an admiral's flag. But an array of decorations made up for that: 15 service medals, including the Param Vishisht Seva Medal. He retired as director-general, naval dockyard, Bombay. No medals or trophies adorned the shelves of his home. He passed away in October 1999.

Rear Admiral Satyindra Singh AVSM
Commissioned in Indian Navy in 1941
Satyindra Singh was born at Lahore on 23RD May 1920. He studied at Forman Christian College, Lahore. After graduation, then the Second World War caused him to abandon plans for further studying, and he joined the Armed Forces. Commissioned in the Royal Indian Navy Volunteer Reserve in June 1941, he was seconded to Royal Indian Navy, later Indian Navy.

Admiral Satyindra Singh was one of the few staff officers of the Indian Navy who had played a positive role during the Division of the Navy in the wake of Partition.

He was specially selected to assist Admiral Sir Geoffrey Miles and earned praise for his cool and measured response to problems that beset that office at Partition of the Indian subcontinent. In the Navy, he served on the warships - the cruisers *INS Delhi*, *INS Mysore* and the aircraft carrier, *INS Vikrant*, and various shore establishments, including *INS Hamla*. He was posted at the Indian High Commission in London in the period 1949 to 1951.

Indian Navy

Rear Admiral Satyindra Singh AVSM
In 1953 he went for the Coronation Review to UK and was one of the only two Indian Naval officers to be awarded the Coronation Medal. He qualified at the prestigious inter-services Defence Services Staff College Course in Wellington and also the National Defence College Course. For 11 years, till retiring in 1977, he held senior appointments in the military and intelligence wing of the Cabinet Secretariat and later became member secretary of the Joint Intelligence Committee. He passed away on July 18TH 2000.

Rear Admiral, Balwant Singh PVSM
Commissioned in Indian Navy in 1942
Sardar Balwant Singh was commissioned in the Royal Indian Navy in September 1942. He was born in the village Pandoori Ran Singh, one of the historic five Pandoori villages founded by Baba Buddha Singh Randhawa, in Tarn Taran, district Amritsar. Belonging to a family with an Armed Forces heritage going back several generations, he was the son of a First World War veteran, Sardar Surain Singh Randhawa, who had served in various campaigns on the North West Frontier, in Mesopotamia, and Europe. On completion of his schooling in Penang, where he excelled as a bright student and in athletics, as a fast bowler and as a hockey centre forward, he graduated from the Panjab University and thereafter was selected for Commissioned Officers' Training for the Indian Army, in the Indian Military Academy at Dehradun. While he was under training, the Government issued a call for volunteers for commission in the Royal Indian Navy, which was being expanded to meet the war plans of the Allied powers.

Indian Navy

Rear Admiral, Balwant Singh PVSM

He voluntccred and thereafter never had time to look back. Immediately on commissioning in 1942, while Second World War was in full slate, he was appointed to sea on *HMIS Barracuda*, a light Frigate deployed in the Bay of Bengal for keeping the sea route open for Calcutta. While on patrol duties he saw action against Japanese air strikes. For these active war operations he received the George VI 39-45 Medal, the Burma Star, and the 1939-45 Star. After the war he was appointed to the Naval Establishment *HMIS Hamla* at Bombay and was one of the few Indian Officers, serving alongside many British counterparts.

The Naval Sailors Mutiny erupted on 18TH February 1946 as a consequence of poor service conditions, the racially biased behaviour of some British Officers and the delays associated with demobilization and resettlement of Indian Sailors after Second World War. During this critical situation, with nationalist sentiments also running high, (then) Lieutenant Commander Balwant Singh played a pivotal role in calming and re-assuring the agitated Indian Sailors of *HMIS Hamla* by winning their confidence, preventing escalation of the situation and restoring order, thereby avoiding harm to British personnel and their families. However, while deposing before the commission set up to determine the cause, extent and consequences of the Naval Mutiny, he had the courage of conviction to state that there were innumerable cases of racial discrimination in the RIN which made the lot of Indian Officers serving under some British Officers very miserable. Events moved rapidly towards independence of the country, and Indian Naval Officers took up the challenge to fill the places vacated by the British Royal Navy Officers.

Indian Navy

Rear Admiral, Balwant Singh PVSM

In 1946, he was appointed as Officer-in-Charge, RIN Pay Office, at a time when post-war demobilization and settlement of accounts was at its peak. He was promoted to the rank of Commander in 1948, and being the first 'turbaned' Sikh Officer to rise to that rank; he played a leading role in designing the "brass hat" for the "naval turban badge". In 1952, he was appointed as the Supply Officer of the Indian Navy's flagship, *INS Delhi*. He was jointly the Flotilla Supply Officer, and was responsible for all the logistic, secretarial, financial and legal matters of the entire Fleet. He was also a Member of the Indian contingent at the Coronation of Queen Elizabeth II and received the Queen Elizabeth II Coronation Medal. In 1955 he was promoted to Captain and appointed as Director of Stores at Naval Headquarters, New Delhi. Rear Admiral Balwant Singh was instrumental in laying the foundation of the Naval Stores Organization. In this capacity he put into place the organization and procedures for provisioning, procurement, and supply of Naval and Air stores. In 1962 he was selected to undergo the prestigious National Defence College course, after which he was appointed as the Director of Supply Branch at the Naval Headquarters. In March 1968, the Western Naval Command was created, with the Western Fleet integral to it. Commodore Balwant Singh was appointed as the first Chief Staff Officer, Personnel and Administration, to the Flag Officer Commanding-in-Chief, Western Naval Command. In February 1969, he was promoted to the rank of Rear Admiral and appointed as the first incumbent to the newly created Principal Staff Officer post of Chief of Logistics at Naval Headquarters.

Indian Navy

Rear Admiral, Balwant Singh PVSM
He set the course for the new organization, putting in place effective processes and methods for efficient functioning and meeting the needs of a growing Navy and was decorated by the President with the Param Vishisht Seva Medal for his Distinguished Services. He retired from service in 1970, and settled in New Delhi and was on the UN panel of experts. He passed away in February 1985, after a brief illness. His naval legacy is carried on by his son, Vice Admiral Birinder Singh Randhawa, PVSM, AVSM, VSM, who joined the Indian Navy and rose to become the Chief of Material of the Indian Navy.

Rear Admiral Kirpal Singh, AVSM, ADC
Commissioned in the Royal Navy 1939
Sardar Kirpal Singh, the son of Partap Singh and Laj Wanti, was born on 5TH September 1925 in Beawar, in the district of Ajmer, Rajasthan. Kirpal Singh received his early education at Khalsa High School in Rawalpindi. In 1939, he was selected for a scholarship to join the Indian Mercantile Marine Training Ship *Dufferin* at Bombay. In 1943 he was selected for the Royal Indian Navy and was sent to England for training with the Royal Navy during 1944-45. From September 1945 to March 1946, Singh attended technical courses as a Sub Lieutenant with the Royal Navy.

A year later, he was sent to the UK to specialize in Gunnery at the Royal Navy's Gunnery School at HMS *Excellent*. He served as Midshipman onboard Royal Navy Battleships *H.M.S. Anson* and *King George V.*

Indian Navy

Rear Admiral Kirpal Singh, AVSM, ADC

He saw active service in World War Two, first in the Atlantic and Arctic Oceans against Germany and later in the Pacific Ocean against the Japanese.

On return to India he served in several ships and establishments and later commanded Indian Naval Ships *Ganga, Tir, Brahmaputra, Beas, the aircraft carrier Vikrant* and the Western Fleet. His shore appointments included: A.D.C. to the first Indian Governor General, C. Rajagopalachari, Officer in Charge Gunnery School, Battalion Commander at the National Defence Academy, Khadakvasla (Pune), and Deputy Naval Adviser to Indian High Commissioner to U.K. He was appointed Chief of Personnel at Naval Headquarters, and Commodore in Charge Naval Barracks at Bombay and Director General Naval Dockyard Expansion Scheme, Bombay.

He is a Graduate of the Defence Services Staff College, Wellington, Nilgiris, the Joint Services Staff College, U.K. and the prestigious Royal College of Defence Studies, London. He was awarded the Ati Vishisht Seva Medal for his contribution to the Human Resource Development in the Indian Navy. In 1949, Kirpal Singh served as Aide de Camp to India's first Governor General, Mr C. Rajagopalachari. He held many positions during his naval career. He commanded various ships and establishments, including the aircraft carrier *INS Vikrant* and the Western Fleet. He retired from the Indian Navy on 31ST March 1977, in the rank of Rear Admiral. Kirpal Singh provided a grant for the launch of the Maritime Museum in Kochi.

Indian Navy

Rear Admiral Jagmohan Singh Sodhi, AVSM, VSM (Retd).

Commissioned in the Indian Navy in 1961
Jagmohan Singh Sodhi was born on 11TH September 1939 at Digri, Sind (now in West Pakistan) and his parents were Sardar Amar Singh Sodhi and Mrs. Leela Sodhi. He was the eldest child and was followed by four more brothers and one sister. After his initial schooling at Digri, he was sent to Saint Marys High School, Mount Abu in the state of Rajasthan in March 1945 where he studied in the boarding school till 1952. His parents lived in a joint family which had considerable fertile land holdings as well as substantial immovable property.

Saint Marys School was a very prestigious school and all the princes of Rajasthan Royal families used to study there and the class strength used to be very limited.

After partition of India into two states on 15TH August 1947 the family had to move out and since they had nowhere to go they shifted to Mount Abu as the eldest son and his cousin were studying and where the Government was kind enough to give them shelter in the Panchayat House. In 1952 the Government of India allotted the family 100 acres of agricultural land in Village Jugian Man Singh on the banks of River Sutlej near Phillaur (Punjab) and therefore the family had to move to their own house in Ludhiana in Punjab which was only 13 miles from the village. The main problem was admission in the new schools as the school curriculum was very different and class V standard was not found equivalent to any Indian class standard.

Indian Navy

Rear Admiral Jagmohan Singh Sodhi

He studied for Metric Examination (10TH class) and in May 1954 qualified in the Metric examination in first Division, which was a great achievement from 5TH class to 10TH class in 15 months. In 1955 Jagmohan applied for the National Defence Academy (NDA) Examination and was selected as a Naval Cadet to join NDA in July 1956 with the 16TH NDA course. He did quite well in the NDA and in the 6TH term he was appointed as the Battalion Cadet Captain and joined INS Tir, the cadet training ship for sea training in July 1959. He was later transferred to INS Mysore as Midshipmen in January 1960 where he served as Fleet navigating Officers Doggy for some months as also the Senior Midshipmen in the 16TH course for two months. On commissioning on 1ST January, 1961 the course had to go for Sub. Lieutenants training at various schools at Kochi and other establishments and again he did very well in all the courses. Thereafter he did short stints on *Khukri* and *Kirpan* and after award of watch keeping ticket was appointed as Executive Officer of *INS Bimlipatnam,* an ocean going minesweeper. In 1963 he was appointed as watch keeping officer on board the aircraft carrier *INS Vikrant*. In 1964 Lieutenant Sodhi was selected for Submarine training at *HMS Dolphin* in United Kingdom. This was the period when there was considerable racism in the UK and the RN officers had prepared a tote as to which country's students would do the best in the submarine examinations and the odds for Indians was 1:25.

Indian Navy

Rear Admiral Jagmohan Singh Sodhi

These were soon proved wrong as we did quite well. After completion of submarine training in 1965, Jagmohan was appointed in Command of the Customs ship *INS Suvarna*. After the refusal by Western powers to sell a modern submarine to the Indian Navy, the Indian Government approached the then Soviet Union for submarines, and they were more than willing. Thus in February 1966 all UK trained submariners and some new comers were assembled at *INS Angre* for Russian Language training and on 22ND June 1966 the main and spare crew of the first Indian submarine landed at Vladivostok for training under the Soviet system.

On 8TH December 1967 the first Indian Naval submarine *INS Kalvari* was commissioned at Riga and Lt. JMS Sodhi was the commissioning Commander of the Battle Department III or the Torpedo Officer. After extensive work up including weapon firings the submarine sailed around South Africa to arrive at its base in Vishakhapatnam in July 1968 when the foundation stone of the Naval Dockyard Vishakhapatnam and the Integrated Submarine Complex of *INS Virbahu* and *Satavahana* was laid by the Chief of Naval Staff. In August 1969 Lt. JMS Sodhi was selected to be the commissioning Executive Officer of India's fourth submarine *INS Kursursa* and since the majority of the crew were fresher's it was an herculean task to mould the ships company into a cohesive fighting force and for these efforts Lt. JMS Sodhi was awarded the Vishist Seva Medal in 1971.

Indian Navy

Rear Admiral Jagmohan Singh Sodhi

On 19TH January 1969 Lt. JMS Sodhi married Miss Meena Bakshi, daughter of Mr. and Mrs. Darshan Singh Bakshi who was also a famous landlord in Sind and even had a small town Darshannagar named after him. The couple was blessed with one son 1971 and the second son in 1972 and both the children are happily settled in the USA with two kids each.

During 1971 Lt. JMS Sodhi was busy setting up the training department in *INS Virbahu* as *INS Satavahana* was still not ready and various syllabi were prepared which proved quite useful once Satavahana took over the submarine training. In April 1972 Lt. Cdr, JMS Sodhi was appointed in Command of *INS Kursursa* which was then operating off Mumbai and was able to fire six practice torpedoes in a single day which was then a record of sorts. In May 1973 Lt. Cdr. JMS Sodhi was deputed to USSR to witness the deep diving trials of the first of the new Vela class submarines which he later commissioned as Commanding Officer on 31ST August 1973. The submarine was based at Mumbai and thus the 9TH submarine squadron was formed at Mumbai on the lines of the 8TH submarine squadron at Vishakhapatnam.

In the meantime the Indian Navy was looking for ways to develop its own submarine manufacturing facilities and acquisition of submarines from sources other than the Soviet Union and for this purpose the Naval Headquarters required special officers to steer the project. Accordingly Commander JMS Sodhi was appointed to NHQ as Deputy Director of Submarine Arm in August 1975.

Indian Navy

Rear Admiral Jagmohan Singh Sodhi

However, soon a requirement came up to replace the Commanding Officer of *INS Kalvari* which was undergoing major refit in the Soviet town of Vladivostok and Cdr. JMS Sodhi was deputed to the USSR in early 1976 to Command *INS Kalvari* and after the refit bring her back to India. After arrival at Vishakhapatnam in September 1976 Cdr. JMS Sodhi was posted back to his old job as Deputy Director of Submarine Arm at Naval Headquarters. At this stage the Director of the Submarine Arm was a non submariner namely Captain Madhu Kondath and therefore the appointment of his Deputy was very critical for the development of the submarine arm.

The Project for the acquisition of SSK submarines proceeded at a very fast pace and by 1979 the contract was signed for the acquisition of two submarines from Germany and for the indigenous construction of two submarines at Mazagaon Docks Mumbai.

In May 1980 Commander JMS Sodhi was appointed as Commanding Officer *INS Virbahu* and Captain (SM) of the 8TH Submarine Squadron at Vishakhapatnam. During this period the first ever medium repair of Indian submarine was completed by the Naval Dockyard Vishakhapatnam and when the submarine *Khandheri* sailed for the deep diving trials not a single defect was noticed. This was in great contrast to the medium repairs of the surface ship *INS Kadmatt* which broke down at sea and had to be towed back to harbour. The submarine class authority *INS Virbahu* played a very positive role in overseeing the refit of submarines.

Indian Navy

Rear Admiral Jagmohan Singh Sodhi

In May 1982 Captain JMS Sodhi was appointed Captain P31 which for the first time comprised of 10 vessels as the 32 Patrol Vessel Squadron of 5 vessels based at Mumbai were also transferred to Vishakhapatnam to be part of 31 Patrol Vessel Squadron. In May 1983 Captain JMS Sodhi was appointed Director of Submarine Arm at Naval Headquarters. In the period 1983-84 he visited USSR as part of Defence Secretary Delegation where contract for 10 8777 EKM class submarines was signed. The next few years saw our submarines operating in the Atlantic, Pacific and Indian Ocean.

In January, 1985 Captain JMS Sodhi was the first submariner to be selected for the National Defence College and next year he was appointed in Command of the Submarine Depot ship *INS Amba*. On completion of his Command in May 1987 he was appointed as Commanding Officer of *INS Vagravahu* and Commodore Commanding Submarines (West). In August 1988 he was promoted to Flag Rank and appointed as Flag Officer Submarines at Vishakhapatnam.

The concept of Operational Readiness Inspection as was in vogue with the Fleet Air Arm was also adopted for submarine squadrons and this was .quite beneficial for submarine operational readiness. In April 1991 Rear Admiral JMS Sodhi was appointed as Senior Directing staff at National Defence College at New Delhi from where he retired from the Navy on 30TH September 1993 at the age of 54.

Indian Navy
Naval College Dartmouth

Britannia Royal Naval College (BRNC) the initial officer training establishment of the Royal Navy, located on a hill overlooking Dartmouth, Devon, England. Delivering learning that is inspiring, challenging and relevant to meet Fleet operational capability. It has been at the forefront of the education and development of world-class Naval Officers in Dartmouth since 1863.

It would appear that Indian cadets trained at Dartmouth from May 1939 and this continued after WW2. 1947 was a tumultuous year with partition and the splitting of the Navy between India and Pakistan, followed by slow consolidation. Only in 1948, when things had settled down, was the first batch sent to Dartmouth. Indian Navy Cadets stopped training Dartmouth when in 1955 and the Indian Navy had set up training schools in Cochin. The training was undertaken in India from 1955 onwards.

(Against tremendous odds the information about Sikh naval officers that trained at Dartmouth was obtained by Vice Admiral Harinder Singh (Retd), Indian Navy.

Indian Navy

Vice Admiral Inderjit Singh Khurana PVSM (Retd)
Commissioned from Dartmouth in 1948

Admiral Khurana was born to an illustrious family in April 1930 and was commissioned in the in 1948. He obtained his basic five years training at the British Naval Institutions, in the United Kingdom including Dartmouth. He is a graduate of the Defence Services Staff College, Wellington, where he subsequently served as the Chief Instructor (Navy). His career profile in the Navy comprised of numerous commands, administrative and staff assignments Vice Admiral I.S. Khurana retired from the Indian Navy after 39 years of unblemished and distinguished service for which he received the highest service award of Param Vishist Seva Medal.

The officer in his last decade of his service held top managerial posts both afloat and ashore. He retired as the Director General Coast Guard. Prior to this appointment he commanded both the Eastern and Western Fleets of the Indian Navy, in succession, a rare distinction in itself.

His other assignments in Flag rank was that of Chief of Staff, Eastern Naval Command where he was charged with the responsibilities of development of shore support facilities and administration and training of a large number of men.

In February, 1985 he was appointed as the Director General Coast Guard. He was instrumental in the induction of number of vessels and aircraft and commissioning of Coast Guard shore and air stations thus making the Indian Coast Guard a strong and viable paramilitary force with an all-India capability.

Indian Navy

Vice Admiral Inderjit Singh Khurana PVSM (Retd)
He twice served as Director in Naval Headquarters and preformed the duties of planning of futuristic projects and establishment of civil and harbour works ashore. From 1973 to 1977 he was posted as Indian Naval Attaché at the Embassy of India in Moscow and concurrently accredited to Poland.

As Naval Attaché, he established close personal rapport with senior Defence officers' especially senior Soviet Naval officers; in the Ministry of Defence and the State Committee of Economic Relations of the then USSR Government In discharge of his official duties he has had frequent interaction with top Soviet entrepreneurs, designers and manufacturers of defence equipment.

He is now happily settled with his wife and family in New Delhi.

Commodore Harbans Singh Punia
Commissioned from Dartmouth in 1949
Harbans Singh Punia was born in Village Nagra in Jalandhar District. His father was in the judicial service and often moved from place to place where his duties took him. Some of the important early years were spent in Rajasthan and his education was in Ludhiana.

He joined the Navy at Kochi in March 1949 and after three weeks of orientation he sailed for London, Tilbury docks and arrived after a 20 day passage. He joined RNC Dartmouth for 3 months training in a group of about 200 comprising others from South Africa, Australia, Pakistan, Egypt, and Iran etc.

Indian Navy

Commodore Harbans Singh Punia

As a midshipman he served on various ships including the aircraft carriers *Indomitable* and *Implacable* and then returned to RNC Greenwich grounding in the newly opened fields of Sonar, Radar etc. On completion he joined *INS Mysore* at Spithead for the fleet review of 1953 and thereafter served on *Talwar* and *Rajput* for a couple of years.

He then went back to UK for the special weapons course – after serving as the Squadron Gunnery Officer of the Hunt Class destroyers and back to Mysore as the GO in 1958 and thence to the Rajput Class as the Squadron GO.

During the India–China conflict of 1962 he was the second in command on board *INS Talwar* and the ship was tasked to patrol the Andaman's and the India-Indonesia border and keep them safe. At the time of the 1965 Indo-Pak war he was at the DSSC, Wellington.

In the subsequent years he served as the Staff Gunnery Officer to C-in-C East, Commanding Officer *Rajput*, Instructor at the DSSC, Wellington, Commanding Officer Amba, Director at IDM and *CO Mysore* was his last sea command. His ship handling prowess on Mysore was exemplary and the best the navy had seen.

His final appointment in the navy before he decided to retire was as the Director of Acquisition Project where he was responsible for major acquisitions of ships and submarines fro Soviet Union in multimillion dollar deals that built the foundation of the current Navy. He retired in 1979 and settled down in Delhi.

Indian Navy

Commodore JMS Sood, AVSM (Retd)
Commissioned at Dartmouth in 1949

Commodore Jag Mohan Singh Sood was born on 24TH July, 1929 in Lahore, in undivided India. His early education was in Lahore where he did his Matriculation from Rang Mahal Mission High School. He was studying in BSc (Hons) when the Partition of India occurred and his family fled to India to escape the carnage in Lahore. Thus, his college education was cut short. On arrival in India his family became refugees staying in different cities till they settled in Lucknow. He joined the Indian Navy as an officer cadet in October 1948 and proceeded to UK where he trained at the Royal Naval College, Dartmouth, in 1949. He served on board Royal Navy ships which visited a large number of countries particularly Japan, Korea and Singapore. He was commissioned into the Indian Navy on 1ST March 1951 in the Supply and Secretariat Branch. He served in the National Defence Academy, Khadakvasla. During 1956-1959 he was Instructor in Naval Training Team. From October 1962 to March 1965 he was deputed as Deputy Controller of Stores & Purchases to Heavy Engineering Corporation, Ranchi for a period of 2 years and 4 months. He was deputed to Canteen Stores Department as Vice Chairman in October 1973 where he served with distinction for 5 years. During this period he officiated as Chairman of CSD for 8 months. In November 1978 he reverted back to the Navy. His most prestigious naval appointment was as Director of Supply Branch from November 1978 to May 1982.

Indian Navy

Commodore JMS Sood, AVSM (Retd)

He was awarded the Ati Vishist Seva Medal on 26 January 1982. Commodore Sood hung up his sword on 31ST May 1982 and has had a fruitful second innings. He was associated with 2 Commissions of Inquiry set up post 1984 anti-Sikh riots. He is married to a Maharashtra lady doctor Mrs. Kusum Sood; she served in the Indian Navy for 10 years and retired as a Surgeon Lieutenant Commander. She was awarded the Vishist Sewa Medal for her dedicated service in the 1971 war. The Soods have the rare distinction as a naval family wherein both the husband and wife were awarded AVSM and VSM for distinguished service.

Commander Hardev Singh NM (Retd.)

Trained at Dartmouth and Commissioned in 1953

Commander Hardev Singh was born in Rawalpindi on July 29TH, 1933 to Mr. Prahlad Singh, who was then serving in the army.

He joined Indian Military Academy, Dehradun, as a naval cadet and underwent training from January 1949 to December 1950. On completion he joined *INS Venduruthy* for training at Kochi from January 1951 to March 1951. He was then deputed to UK for training at RNC Dartmouth & HMS Devonshire from April 1951 to April 1952. He returned to India and underwent Sea Training as Midshipman / Sub-Lieutenant on *INS Tir, Delhi, Jumna & Rana* from April 1952 to December 1953 and was commissioned as a Sub Lieutenant in the Indian Navy on 1ST September 1953.

Indian Navy

Commander Hardev Singh NM (Retd.)

He returned to UK and underwent continued training at RNC Greenwich & Tech Courses at Portsmouth / Plymouth, etc from January 1954 to July 1955. He then served on *INS Bimlipatam* from July 1955 to March 1956 and *INS Delhi & Ganga* from March 1956 to March 1957. He went to Cranwell in UK for flying training with the Royal Air Force from 1957 to March 1958. He then joined the 550 Squadron at Cochin from March 1958 to December 1960. He joined INAS 310, an Indian Air Squadron, in France in December 1960, and was present when INAS 310 was commissioned on 21ST March 1961 at Hyeres, St. Raphel by the Indian Ambassador to France. In April 1961, back in UK, he participated in the first deck landing carried out on *INS Vikrant,* off Yeovilton, in Alize 203. In the same month the Cobras participated in their first tactical exercise with *INS Betwa* and *INS Beas*, which were sailing to India from the UK. He commanded the Air squadron, in INAS 310 on board *INS Vikrant* when on 18TH August 1961 it sailed back to India via the Suez Canal. The squadron was initially based at *INS Garuda,* and saw operational action on 18TH December 1961 and during Operation Vijay for the liberation of Goa. From March 1964 to June 1965 he served as the Air Operation Officer on *INS Vikrant*. From June 1965 to April 1967 he served at the Naval Headquarters as Deputy Director Sailing, Naval Academy. From April 1967 to December 1967 he attended a Staff Course at Defence Services Staff College at Wellington.

Indian Navy

Commander Hardev Singh NM (Retd.)
From December 1967 to 1969 he served as an Executive Officer on INS Rajput and from January 1969 to March 1971 he served as a Command Aviation Officer, WNC, Bombay. From March 1971 to December 1972 he was Commanding Officer and Commander 22 Destroyer Squadron on *INS Godavari*. From December 1972 to September 1975 he served as Joint Planning Staff (Navy) Cabinet, Secretary, New Delhi.

He was awarded the Nao Sena Medal Awarded during the 1971 Indo-Pak war and Sainya Seva Medal with Clasp, Andaman & Nicobar.

He retired at his own request in March 1976.

Commodore T.S. Khurana (NM)
Commissioned at Dartmouth in 1953
Trilochan Singh was born in Rawalpindi on 16TH November 1933. He did his Kindergarten and up to grade 5 in the Presentation Convent, thereafter, a boarder in St Joseph's Convent Dehradun. He was selected for the erstwhile Prince of Wales Military College (now Rashtriya Indian Military College) Dehradun, where he passed the Senior Cambridge with distinction, in August 1948. He was then selected for the First (pioneer) Course of JSW in Dehradun, (now the National Defence Academy, Khadakvasla), opting for the Indian Navy and passed out in December 1950. Since no facilities then existed for training naval cadets in India, the batch of 19 naval cadets sailed to the UK, to be trained with the Royal Navy for 5 years.

Indian Navy

Commodore T.S. Khurana (NM)
This training started with the Royal Naval College Dartmouth (in Devon) and continued with the training cruiser, Royal Naval College Greenwich and culminated with the professional courses in various specialist establishments of the Royal Navy. He was commissioned as Acting-sub-lieutenants on 1ST September 1953.

On being promoted to the rank of a Lieutenant, he obtained 'Watch keeping Certificate' qualifying him to hold independent charge of all types of ships at sea. Navigated (as a non-specialist) IN ships *Bengal*, *Ganga* and *Rana*. He took part in various joint sea exercises with other navies of the Commonwealth countries in 1956 and 1957. He then specialised in Navigation and direction (control of aircraft on board an aircraft carrier) in Cochin. On completion, selected as advance crew for the first aircraft carrier being refurbished for the Indian Navy, *INS Vikrant* in Belfast, 2 years prior to her commissioning. On Vikrant's commissioning, in February 1962, served another 3 years on board. Thereafter, served as the senior instructor Navigation and Direction School, Cochin and later appointed as the Navigating Officer of the flagship *INS Delhi*, based in Bombay.

Command of ships /squadrons:
1. INS Kirpan-won the Fleet Proficiency Trophy (Western Fleet). 2. INS Trishul-just converted to a missile frigate - visited Seychelles and East African ports on a goodwill cruise -with the flagship. Concurrently, Squadron Commander 15TH Frigate Squadron.

Indian Navy

Commodore T.S. Khurana (NM)
3. Squadron Commander 25TH Missile boat squadron (known as the "killer squadron" because of their deadly attack on Karachi in December, 1971) the squadron comprised of 16 operational vessels.

During the Indo-Pak war, December 1971, he was the Fleet Navigating Officer and planned and executed Operations Trident & Python - attacks on Karachi. He was awarded the Nao Sena Medal for gallantry, courage and dedication.

Staff Appointments:
1. He was, Deputy Director Weapon Policy and Tactics- Naval Headquarters as a Commander. Was the Deputy leader of a high level deputation which visited various countries in Europe, including the UK to select weapons and sensors for the new Leander Class frigates being indigenously built. All the recommendations were accepted by the Ministry of Defence and the Government.
2. He was Director of Naval Plans Naval HQ, as a captain for 1 year.

Inter-Services Appointments:
1. He served as President of Services Selection Board and Commander Selection Centre for 3 years.
2. He was Vice Chairman and Joint General Manager Canteen Stores Department, Mumbai for 3 years, and officiated as Chairman for the last 6 months. He was awarded Commendation by the CNS.

Indian Navy

Commodore T.S. Khurana (NM)

Command Appointments:
Chief of Staff: Was the Chief of Staff and CSO (operations) Eastern Naval Command for 3 years. Before retiring from the Navy on 30TH May 1987, was appointed the Chief of Staff and CSO (operations) in the Western Naval Command, Mumbai for 18 months.

He attended:
Junior Staff Course, Royal Naval College, Greenwich.
Advanced work study in Llandour, Mussoorie
He attended Adolescent human psychology and Interview technique in Army Headquarters and Defence Services Staff College, Wellington.

Sports
Represented JSW/Royal Navy /Indian Navy/ Inter-services hockey teams.

Post-Retirement Work Experience (1987 – 2014):
June 1987-Jan 1988-Deputy Director General Coastguard New Delhi.
June 1988 – May 1992 - CEO of Eagle Flasks.
June 1992 – June 1995 - Sumeet Machines.
August 1995–May 2014-President of the AARJAY Group of companies, Mumbai.

He retired in 2014 to settle down in Chandigarh.

Indian Navy

Commodore M.S. Ratra, VSM
Commissioned at Dartmouth in 1953

Commodore Mankeshwar Singh Ratra was born to a landed family in Dalhousie in the undivided Punjab on 18TH May 1932 and received his early education in Punjab. He decided that his future lay at sea and he joined *TS Dufferin* for the merchant marine in January 1947 and was selected to join the Indian Navy as was the practise for those who did well on the training ship in their last year. He joined Dartmouth as a cadet in January 1950 doing one term on board *Devonshire* and then two terms on board two cruisers, each in the North Sea and the Mediterranean.

On promotion as a midshipman he was posted to Malta on board submarine depot ship *HMS Forth*, which cared for 8 T Class submarines. On promotion to the rank of Sub Lieutenant he was assigned to *HMS Lochscheibe*. He then joined *RNC Greenwich* for his Sub Lieutenants courses for 2 terms and also participated in the coronation review in 1953. He was attached to various schools including Davenport, Collinwood etc and returned to India in March 1954 and was appointed to *INS Tir*. Here looked after the training of cadets from the 5TH to the 9TH courses. He was appointed as the XO of an SPC that did much sailing and patrolled the India – Goa boundary prior to the liberation of Goa.

He then returned back to UK for his Long Gunnery course at the Gunnery School, Chatham. On completion of the course he requested permission to return overland as the Suez was closed.

Indian Navy

Commodore M.S. Ratra, VSM

He returned to India having traversed many countries by train including France, East and West Germany, Poland, USSR, Turkmenistan till the Afghanistan border, finally flying to Delhi from Kabul – all in 6 weeks. He was then the training co-ordinater in B&D School and recced the setting up of the then sailors Training School at Goa. He then served on board *Rajput*, *Trishul* and *Mysore* and ashore in *Trata* before being appointed AS. In 1969 he was selected to proceed to Russia to commission *INS Kavaratti*. After Kavaratti tenure he served as the Command Operations and Plans Officer, Eastern Naval Command. He was Commander *INS Circars* till 1972 end and was then sent back to NHQ as the first Jt Director of Intelligence at NHQ. He was then appointed as the Director Acquisition Project where he served with distinction from 1974 to 1978 and was responsible for the induction of many ex-Soviet Acquisitions in the Indian Navy. He travelled several times to the Soviet Union for negotiations. He then moved to the Indian Coast Guard as in the rank of IG before it was set up and served as the Deputy Director General from 1978 to 1990 and over saw the setting up of the Coast Guard and to grow it to a sizable force. He did sterling work and was decorated for the same. For his services he was awarded the VSM and Tatrakshak (Coast Guard) Medal.

Indian Navy

The following is the experiences of the Sikh naval officers in Dartmouth in 1951:-

After passing out from JSW, Trilochan Singh Khurana, Rajinder Singh Grewal, Hardev Singh, and Harbhajan Singh, were amongst the Indian Naval cadets that were trained at Dartmouth in England. On the morning of 17TH March 1951, they boarded the P & O liner *SS Strathaid* at Bombay and after nearly a month's memorable voyage; they landed in Tilbury, England. Their term at Dartmouth lasted from May to August 1951. When Admiral of the Fleet Lord Louis Mountbatten visited Dartmouth, the Indian cadets adorned the entire Front rank of the Guard of Honour, on merit, as we were by far the smartest cadets on board.

They boarded the *HMS Devonshire*, a Training Cruiser, and undertook the Autumn Cruise to the Mediterranean ports like Gibraltar, Syracuse (Sicily), Sorrento (off Naples), Malta, Rhode Island of Greece etc. Here they were taught to undertake all the chores of a sailor as well as class room instructions for professional subjects in running a warship. The cruise lasted from end September to December 1951 and after a brief break, they undertook winter cruise (end January 1952 to end March 1952) took them to the West Indies, where they were to visit ports, home to 'rum and coca cola' and 'steel bands' such as Port of Spain in Trinidad, Grenada, St Lucia, Antigua, British Virgin Island and Bermuda etc. May 1952 saw them returning to India on board *SS Circassia* of Anchor Line, a grand holiday on board for over three weeks.

Indian Navy

Also on First May they were promoted to the rank of Midshipman, a strange rank that hung between a sailor and an officer. They joined *INS Tir*, the very first Training Frigate of the Navy and were the very first trainees.

They remained in *INS Tir* for only 8 months as midshipmen. Thereafter they were distributed amongst various ships of the Fleet for another 8 months, and undertook the Mediterranean Cruise with the rest of the Fleet, visiting exotic places such as Malta, Naples, Dubrovnik and Split in Yugoslavia, Corfu etc.

On First of September, 1953 they received our first stripe and became Sub-Lieutenants. Then after serving in various ships they returned to the UK by yet another liner and reached Royal Naval College at Greenwich (London) in December 1953 and stayed on in the UK till May 1955.

After Greenwich they spent a few months doing courses in the naval professional subjects, these took them around the Southern Coast of Britain where these professional schools were located. Once again they were on board another liner to go back home. On arriving at Port Said they were informed that they had to go to Cairo to await the arrival of their Fleet as there had been a collision between two ships and the fleet had returned to Bombay for repairs.

They were also lionized by the Egyptian Military as it was the beginning of the era of Nehru-Nasser friendship and World Military games were in progress then. On return they joined the various arms of the Indian Navy.

British Armed Forces

Lieutenant Colonel Tarlochan Singh Marwaha,
Commissioned at RMAS in 1977

Lieutenant Colonel Marwaha was born on 21ST October 1951 in Nairobi, Kenya and moved to Uganda in 1956. He also represented Uganda in hockey at the U21 level. He left Uganda with his family when Idi Amin, the President of Uganda, ejected all Asians from Uganda in 1972, and settled in UK. He furthered his education by reading for an Electrical Engineering Degree at Liverpool University, graduating as a Bachelor of Engineering (Honours) in 1974. After a short stint working in the civilian market he joined the British Army in 1977. As an Engineer he opted to join the Corps of Royal Electrical and Mechanical Engineers (REME). Following a Commissioning Course at the Royal Military Academy Sandhurst he did various postings as a young Officer, serving in Germany with the British Army of the Rhine (BAOR). During that time he was selected to play hockey for both the Army and the REME. On promotion to Major he did various appointments, the highlight of which was commanding the workshop of 16TH Light Air Defence Regiment, Royal Artillery. Following that he attended a Guided Weapons course at the Royal Military College of Sciences at Shrivenham, gaining a Master of Sciences Degree. This led to a job on guided weapons in the Ministry of Defence in London, followed by a Headquarters Staff Appointment in Germany and then promotion to Lieutenant Colonel.

British Armed Forces

Lieutenant Colonel Tarlochan Singh Marwaha,
As Lieutenant Colonel he had various appointments, some key Staff Appointments in Personnel area and Project Management, and the most enjoyable at the Royal Commissions Board at Westbury, selecting future Officers for the British Army. He finally retired from the Army in April 2012.Throughout his Army career Lt. Col. Marwaha was also actively involved in hockey, as a player, coach and in management. He has played for all his Unit sides, the REME, the Army and the Combined Services teams. He captained and coached his Unit and REME teams. He was the Army coach for several years after he stopped playing at that level and then was Chairman of the Army Hockey Association for several years. During this time he also took up the sport of gliding, at which he represented the Army and competed at the National level. He also took on the responsibility of Chairman of the Army Gliding Association for several years.

Captain Makand Singh
Joined the British Army in 1977
Captain Makand Singh was born in Kuala Lumpar, Malaysia. He studied in India until the age of 14 when he moved with his family to the UK. He enlisted with the Royal Army Ordnance Corps (RAOC) in 1977, at the age of 17. He then became a member of the Royal Logistics Corps when it formed in 1993. During his 33-year army career he was posted in Germany, Belize and Hong Kong. He has represented his Regiment and the army at hockey and coached military and civilian teams.

British Armed Forces

Captain Makand Singh

He has been honoured with the Long Service and Good Conduct medals as well as the prestigious Meritorious Service Medal for his commitment to the recruitment of black and Asian youth into the army. Captain Makand Singh was bestowed with an MBE Award by HRH Queen Elizabeth II in the New Year's Honours list for 2011. He is currently serving as the Regimental Operations Support Officer in a 159 Supply Regiment with Headquarters based in the West Midlands.

Major Sartaj Singh Gogna
Commissioned from RMAS in 2000
Major Sartaj Singh Gogna graduated from Sandhurst in 2000 and joined the Royal Electrical and Mechanical Engineers. He served in Iraq and Afghanistan. He is currently a senior instructor at the School of Royal Electrical and Mechanical Engineering in Arborfield and is Chairman of the British Armed Forces Sikh Association.

Captain (Retd) Harjot Singh Gill
Commissioned from RMAS in 2002
Captain Harjot Singh Gill was initially educated at Brunel University where in 2001 he gained Bachelor of Science (BSc) Mathematics. He was commissioned from Sandhurst Military Academy in May 2002 as 2ND Lieutenant and joined the Royal Logistic Corps. On commissioning Lieutenant Harjot Singh Gill took command of his first troop in Oxfordshire and deployed with them on a tour of Basra and Alamara, Iraq.

British Armed Forces

Captain (Retd) Harjot Singh Gill
Shortly after his return to the UK he deployed to Northern Ireland as a Brigade Staff Officer, where he controlled military assets in a counter-terrorism role in 2005. He was promoted to Captain in late 2006. In 2009, he deployed to the Falklands Islands as Officer Commanding of the Ground Defence Force and again with dual responsibilities as Logistical Second-in-Command. On his return to the United Kingdom in 2010, he was appointed as Communication and Messaging Officer for 4 Mechanized Brigade, a unit that was in preparation to deploy to Afghanistan. In 2013 Captain Harjot Singh Gill took the difficult decision to leave the Army with a view to transit into the private sector. He went on to read an MBA at Brunel Business School in London and has joined one of the world's largest consulting firms. In his spare time he is a British Army Reserve Officer, assisting new soldiers in training. He also takes pride in teaching outdoor skills by organising community hikes.

Second Lieutenant Jagraj Singh
Commissioned from RMAS in 2003
Second Lieutenant Jagraj Singh graduated from The Royal Military Academy Sandhurst to be Lieutenant on 13TH December 2003. He served in the armed forces until December 2006 and left to set up 'Everythings 13' a Sikh educational charity. One of its major projects is "Basics of Sikhi", a youtube channel designed to spread the wisdom of the Sikh Gurus.

British Armed Forces

Captain (Retd) Benjit Singh Dhesi
Commissioned from RMAS in 2005
Benjit Singh Dhesi was born in November 1980 at Banbury, Oxfordshire to Mr. Balbir Singh Dhesi and Mrs. Surinder Kaur Dhesi (Mayor of Banbury Town, 2005). Initially he was educated at Banbury School before attending University College London (UCL), where he gained a degree: BSc (Hons), in Computing and graduated in 2003. He went on to gain: Post-grad: Finance MBA from Manchester Business School (studied in the final year of the Army and when working post-Army), graduated 2012. He was commissioned from Sandhurst Military Academy in April 2005 as 2ND Lieutenant. He was promoted to Captain and left the Army for the City in March 2009. Currently he is Head of Corporate Derivative Sales (Executive Director), Investment Banking, London.

Captain Neil Singh Khepar
Commissioned from RMAS in 2011
Captain Neil Singh Khepar graduated from The Royal Military Academy Sandhurst as a Lieutenant on 16TH April 2011 and joined The Royal Logistic Corps. Currently he is a serving officer in The Royal Logistic Corps.

British Armed Forces

Captain Jagjit Singh Marwaha
Commissioned from RMAS in 2011
Captain Jagjit Singh Marwaha graduated from RMAS on 16TH April 2011 and joined The Royal Regiment of Artillery. In his own words: - "I joined the Regular Army five years ago, having already being part of the Army Reserve. The range of leadership and skills training I have received is something I don't think any civilian employer could match. I recently completed the Fire Support Team Commanders course, which enabled me to move into my current role, commanding a small team of 5-6 soldiers whilst on exercise and operations co-ordinating fires and assets such as attack helicopters onto targets. In my Army career so far, I have been on operational tours to Afghanistan, led exercises in Canada and taken part in light gun fighting in Falklands. But perhaps best of all, being in the Army has allowed me to my pursue passion for hockey. I have toured Belgium, the Netherlands, Gibraltar and most recently Chile, as a part of my Regiment's and the Army's teams". Captain Jagjit Singh Marwaha is currently a serving officer in the British Armed Forces.

Squadron Leader Manjeet Ghataora
Commissioned at Cranwell in 2012
Squadron Leader Majeet Singh Ghataora studied B Eng Aerospace Engineering at University of Hertfordshire. He was commissioned from Cranwell in 2012 and joined 99 Squadron Royal Air Force at Brize Norton. He is currently serving in the 99 Squadron.

British Armed Forces

Lieutenant Brijinder Singh Nijjar
Commissioned from RMAS in 2014
Lieutenant Brijinder Singh Nijjar was born on 6TH August 1991, to Sikh parents who were born in the Punjab, India who now live in Hayes in West London. He read Biology at Royal Holloway before joining the Army. He graduated from The Royal Military Academy Sandhurst in December 2014 and was commissioned into the Army Air Corps as a pilot. He is currently serving with the Army Air Corps.

Lieutenant Harmeet Singh Nijjar
Commissioned from RMAS in 2016
Lieutenant Harmeet Singh Nijjar was born on 1ST September 1992 to Sikh parents who were born in the Punjab, India and now live in Hayes in West London. He read Law at Kingston University before joining the Army. He graduated from The Royal Military Academy Sandhurst in April 2016 and was commissioned into the Army Air Corps as a pilot. He is currently serving with the Army Air Corps.

Navy Lieutenant Sukhdev Singh Cheema
Commissioned in Royal Navy in 2004
Lieutenant Sukhdev Singh Cheema was commissioned on the 1ST July 2004 in the Royal Navy. Currently he is a serving officer. The record shows there are 14 Sikhs serving in the Royal Navy and the Royal Marines today. (2016).

Flight Lieutenant Princejit Singh Ubhi is currently serving in the Royal Air Force.

British Armed Forces (Reserves)

Lieutenant Neel Singh

Neel Singh was born in March 1981. He has been a member of the Royal Navy Reserves for 10 years now and has branched out into the brewing industry with his business Dorking Brewery, a craft brewery based in the heart of the Mole Valley in Surrey.

In his own words:-

'I've been a member of the Royal Naval Reserves for 10 years now. I actually joined after a good friend of mine invited me to a party at BRNC Dartmouth. I signed up the following week! I have done 2 tours of duty, one to UKCC in Bahrain in 2011. I did 7 months there during the Arab Spring so it was quite exciting! My second tour of duty was working for the Commander of the Amphibious Task Group on board *HMS Bulwark* in 2015. I always wanted to be my own boss, so I started my own business brewing beer with the Dorking Brewery!'

Lieutenant Daljinder Singh Virdee

A young Sikh from Hayes has begun a dramatic new path in life after completing the Army Reserve Commissioning Course at the Royal Military Academy in Sandhurst to join 256 (London) Field Hospital Royal Army Medical Corps. Lieutenant Daljinder Singh Virdee, 25, attended Greenford High School in Southall before studying at the University of Reading, graduating with an MPharm in 2012. He is now a Technical Services Pharmacist with Guys Hospital at London Bridge, making a range of specialist drugs and trial treatments.

British Armed Forces (Reserves)

Lieutenant Daljinder Singh Virdee

But he'll now be putting his medical expertise to good use out of office hours in the Army Reserve too, as his new military appointment is as a Pharmacist Officer.

After passing Army Officer Selection in February, Lieutenant Virdee has been busy with his military training at Strensall, near York, before the final 2 weeks at Sandhurst. He said: "It has been an amazing journey so far. I am astounded by the resounding similarities and shared history between the Sikh way of life and the values and standards of the British Army. There were challenges to be met at every corner of the military course which tested both my mental and physical ability & durability, and this left sleep well and truly at the bottom of my list! But I consider it an honour and privilege to have attended the Royal Military Academy Sandhurst". Currently Lieutenant Daljinder Virdee, is a Pharmacist Officer in 256 Field Hospital Royal Army Medical Corps (RAMC) in London.

Flying Officer Ajvir Singh Sandhu

Flying Officer Ajvir Singh Sandhu and Flying Officer Cameron Forster were killed when their aircraft crash landed in a field in North Yorkshire on Saturday 30TH April, 2016. The pair was conducting a privately arranged flight in Slings by Firefly aircraft, hired from the Full Sutton Flying Centre near York.

British Armed Forces (Reserves)

Flying Officer Ajvir Singh Sandhu
Their Squadron Commander, Wing Commander Chris Cartmell, said:-
"All the members of 72 (Reserve) Squadron are deeply saddened by the loss of our close colleagues and friends who were involved in the tragic flying accident on Saturday. Ajvir and Cameron were extremely popular members of our Squadron and their loss will be keenly felt by all. It is very sad that two talented young pilots have been taken from us so early in what would have undoubtedly been highly successful flying careers. Our thoughts are with their families and friends at this difficult time."
Talking about Ajvir their fellow student pilots said:
"Aj was one of the most charismatic members of BFJT, and will be sorely missed by all of us here. An incredibly capable pilot, he would always assist all of us with advice and help anyone who needed it. Alongside this, he was an exceptional friend to everyone and would always fill the bar with laughter at every opportunity. A hard working, talented individual, he summed up everything you'd expect from a trainee fast-jet pilot, and is someone whose qualities we will all strive to emulate."

Appendix

King's commissioned Indian officer

The KCIOs were a category of covenanted officers introduced in the Indian Army at the end of World War 1. Till then the Army was officered entirely by British, and Indians were not given the covenanted status in the Army.

As a result of promises made by the British during World War I, as well as the political pressure for Indianisation of the Army, eleven Viceroy's Commissioned Officers were promoted and granted the King's Commission at the end of the war. By 1923, this figure had risen to twenty three. Some of them were sent for graduation to Royal Military College, Sandhurst. Amongst them was Field Marshal K.M. Carriappa, the first Indian Chief of the Indian Army. However, these promotions meant little as most of the persons promoted were at the fag end of their careers and could not aspire to rise much higher in rank before retirement. In any case, these steps were totally inadequate for the total Indianisation of the officer cadre in the Army and, therefore, it was decided to induct ten officers annually from 1918. At this rate, it would take many years, possibly a century; to Indianise the Army in India and without being Indianised, India could not achieve self-sufficiency or even dominion status. At this time, neither the Navy nor the Air Force existed as part of the Armed Forces of India. So the plan covered only the Army. It was under these circumstances that the first few batches of Indians were sent to the Royal Military College at Sandhurst to be trained as officers.

Appendix

On completion of training, they were to be granted the covenanted King's Commission in the Indian Army. A total of ninety-five officers were commissioned as KCIOs between 1921 and 1933.

The wheels of Indianisation of the Indian Army had been set into motion. The threat from the North, the Third Afghan War, aftermath of the Jallianwala Bagh massacre, the mutiny amongst Indian troops in Jalandhar and Solan in 1920 and the turmoil caused amongst Sikh troops by the Akali Babbar movement in 1920-21 had a cumulative effect resulting in the formation of the Military Requirements Committee called by Lord Rawlinson, the C-in-C in 1921. The Committee proposed the eventual replacement of British by Indian officers, indigenous self-sufficiency, and broadening of the base of all recruitments. They recommended a 25 per cent level of Indianisation with an annual increase. This was not acceptable to Whitehall.

Subsequent deliberations by the India Office resulted in a proposal by the Shea Committee which postulated complete Indianisation of the Army to be carried out in three phases of 14 years each. If the first phase was successful, the second phase could be reduced to nine and subsequently to seven years. From the second phase onwards British officers would cease to be recruited for the Indian Army. The Shea Committee also recommended the establishment of an Indian Military College. Their recommendations were modified and it was agreed to Indianise six infantry Battalions and two cavalry Regiments.

Appendix

Lord Rawlinson also proceeded with opening a pre-Sandhurst institution in the old campus of Imperial Cadet College with a capacity of 27 cadets. The Prince of Wales, later King Edward VIII, formally inaugurated the College on March 13TH 1922. It was being designated the Prince of Wales Royal Indian Military College (RIMC), today's Rashtriya Indian Military College.

In the aftermath of the Third Anglo-Afghan War, there was a need for an increased troop deployment on the Frontier, but the political pressure in the Legislative Assembly demanded a reduction in deployment of troops and curtailment of defence expenditure. Nationalist pressure also increased for the establishment of an Indian "Sandhurst".

Consequently, an Indian Sandhurst Committee was formed in 1926 under Lt. Gen. Sir Andrew Skeen with one British and twelve Indian members. This included Mr. Moti Lal Nehru and Mr. M.A. Jinnah. The committee found that in the previous eight years against 83 vacancies for Indians at Sandhurst 44 had passed successfully. With boys from RIMC joining Sandhurst, the results had improved considerably. The committee recommended that vacancies at Sandhurst be increased gradually to 20 per year till the Indian Sandhurst was established in 1933. An option for training at Royal Military College, Woolwich (Gunners, Engineers), Cranwell (Air force) and Dartmouth (Navy), for entry into arms other than infantry and cavalry continued.

Appendix

The reader might find the excerpt from Maj. Gen. Sukhwant Singh's book 'India's War since Independence', as it appeared titled 'Evolution of Indian Military Concepts' in the Indian Defence Review of 13TH April, 2015, interesting.

Evolution of Indian Military Concept

The Indian Army expanded manifold in World War II to meet the ever-increasing demands of the British contribution to the overall Allied strategy, particularly in West Asia and Southeast Asia.

Drawing on our reservoir of manpower, newly raised units and formations were hurled into battle after short, but nonetheless concentrated, training. The Indian Army of that period was essentially British-led and manpower-oriented. The mechanisation that crept into it was only incidental. Its growth was unbalanced, especially in terms of supporting arms and air complement. On the credit side, Indian troops got an opportunity to fight with first-class armies in different theatres of war from the Western Desert to Italy and from the mountains of Eritrea to the jungles of Burma, shoulder to shoulder with European and US troops. And battle is the best schooling for war.

The tactical concepts of the Indian Army of World War II conformed to the British requirements of the time. Basically, the underlying idea was to trade space for time, initially to allow for equipping and training the formations, and to achieve the requisite build-up so as to turn the tide after completing preparations. It was easy for them as the traded space was in alien lands.

Appendix

In battle, the British believed in a step-by-step deliberate approach with local superiority of at least three to one. The chief protagonist of this concept was Field Marshal Montgomery, but he represented the dictates of the military potential of the wartime armies. The citizen armies were not trained in war manoeuvres and after a series of defeats were hungry for success to tone up national morale. Defeat in battle was unthinkable at that juncture and Montgomery ensured success by creating deliberate and complete superiority over the adversary at a chosen point, and this involved protracted preparations. Surprise and audacity in battle were ignored both in planning and execution, and success solely relied upon the superiority of the blow dealt to the enemy. This was made possible by the free flow of US military aid and the British war industries catching up with defence production. At the end of the war, the bloated Indian Army came home for demobilisation and reduction to suit peacetime colonial requirements in the region. Demobilisation had not been completed when the transfer of power was affected. Nehru's interim government took office, but before it could take stock of future requirements it got entangled in internal dissensions which eventually led to the partition of the country. The government, wedded to the Gandhian philosophy of non-violence, did not take long to spell out the trend of its foreign policy. Nehru made it known that India intended to live in peace with its neighbours and firmly believed that political issues should not be settled by military means.

Appendix

He advocated mutual understanding and cooperation, and preferred negotiations as the main instrument of settlement. This resulted in some misgivings among the rank and file that the army would be drastically cut and that its role would be mainly ceremonial.

While the partitioned armies of India and Pakistan were still busy in dividing assets and escorting refugee caravans, tribal raiders made their way into the Kashmir Valley, blazing a trail of loot, rape and ruthless killings. The outnumbered Jammu and Kashmir forces holding the state border could not beat back the tribal torrent, and they were further weakened by defections in some units. Unable to stem the tide of the invasion, the Maharaja of Kashmir acceded to India, and as a result the responsibility for checking the invaders fell on the Indian Army, then still under a British Commander-in-Chief.

1 Sikh, the nearest unit available, was flown to Srinagar on 26TH October 1947 with the aim of throwing back the raiders. Adequate information about the magnitude of the threat in terms of numbers, weapons and the direction of the thrust was not forthcoming, nor was there time to evaluate in detail the size and composition of the force required to meet it. There were no cohesive units and formations readily available for immediate induction, and as a result units formed by collecting returning elements from Pakistan were dispatched to the Jammu and Kashmir theatre piecemeal.

Appendix

The late Lt. Gen. Kalwant Singh, then a major general and one of the few among the 90 or so King's Commissioned Indian Officers (KCIOs) in service at that time who had held assignments of some consequence, was appointed theatre commander. The initial reaction was to send troops wherever raiders were reported. Operations conformed to the prevalent British mountain warfare tactics, which basically meant piqueting the heights dominating the axes to enable movement of administrative columns along them. The units and formations were led by young Indian officers who as the operations developed grew up with responsibility. Luckily, most of the troops were war veterans and knew the business of war.

A study of the Jammu and Kashmir operations does not reveal any overall strategy either for trapping and destroying the intruders or to block the routes of entry and exit along the state border or even to restore the integrity of these borders. These moves appear to have been expedients to cope with situations as they arose rather than designed to fit into a well-thought-out overall strategy. Two thrusts were developed in the Kashmir Valley, one towards Domel under Brigadier (later Lt. Gen.) L.P. Sen and the other towards Tithwal under Col. (later Lt. Gen.) Harbakhsh Singh. As an offshoot of Sen's offensive, a Battalion under Lt. Col. (later Brigadier) Pritam Singh was inducted in Poonch along the Uri-Haji Pir Pass road. This unit was isolated immediately after induction with the routes leading to Poonch cut off by the raiders on all sides.

Appendix

In other sectors of this little war, operations continued to be directed to link up with the beleaguered Poonch garrison. Poonch was saved because of the indomitable spirit and rare boldness Pritam Singh displayed. He carried out a series of forays deep into enemy–held territory to keep the raiders at bay. Such stunning blows of attrition were inflicted on them that they got scared of the garrison and its commander. But these actions depleted his regular strength to the extent that he had-to fall back on the local militia to meet his ever–growing needs of manpower. Pritam Singh prepared a landing strip for aircraft near the town where Wing Commander Baba Mehar Singh and his men landed to supply the garrison with arms and ammunition and evacuate casualties. As the strip was under enemy artillery fire, landings were mostly at night without proper navigational aids. To feed the garrison and the loyal civil population, Pritam Singh organised harvesting of grain in the surrounding agricultural belts under hostile occupation. The thrust from Jammu to affect a linkup with Poonch met stiff opposition near Jhangar and Kotli and took more time and many more troops than originally estimated. As the war dragged on, the troop build-up increased both north and south of the Pir Panjal range, and this command and control became unmanageable by force headquarters. Accordingly, the force was divided into two Divisions, one north of Pir Panjal under Maj. Gen. (later Gen) Thimayya and the other in the south under the late Maj. Gen. Atma Singh.

Appendix

Kalwant Singh moved out to Army Headquarters as Chief of General Staff and Lt. Gen. Shrinagesh took overall command of the theatre.

The entire Indian Army field force, excluding the minimal holding force, was by now committed in Jammu and Kashmir. Jhangar and Rajauri were secured in the south and a link with Poonch established. Zojila was secured in the north and linked with Leh. Induction of regular Pakistani troops all along the front stiffened resistance, and operations generally stabilised. At that time, international pressures forced a ceasefire on 31 December 1948, and as a result both armies settled down in penny packets to man the ceasefire line in an uneasy eyeball-to-eyeball confrontation under the supervision of the United Nations Military Observer Group for India and Pakistan (UNMOGIP).

Throughout the operations, Baba Mehar Singh and his men provided excellent support, flying day and night in rickety leftover machines of World War II in very hazardous weather and terrain. He had many firsts to his credit. He was the first pilot to land at Leh on a hastily prepared strip at that altitude, to use Dakotas on a bombing raid, and to land at Poonch at night under hostile fire. In fact, wherever there was an air fight Mehar Singh was in the lead, and he became a legend. It goes to Kalwant Singh's credit that he built up the administrative infrastructure from scratch, ensured smooth induction and husbanded his force well.

Appendix

He welded the hastily assembled units and formations into a fighting machine and with his characteristic gruff, no nonsense mannerisms drove it hard. He was at the same time egoistic, positively rude in speech and intolerant of inefficiency, and as a result he made a lot of enemies both within and outside the Army. By no means have a military genius, but certainly a man of iron wills, he kept the force on the continuous offensive against odds and saved two-thirds of Jammu and Kashmir for India.

The Indian Army emerged from these operations as a cohesive fighting force. But it was still infantry-oriented, lacking the balance of supporting arms and administrative services, and equipped with World War II weaponry. It had fought for the first time under Indian commanders and acquitted itself reasonably well, and for this the credit must largely go to the war-tried rank and file and their British training as well as the all-pervading fervour for a national cause.

On the military plane, the operations were confined to the frontier warfare pattern against irregulars and were not of much use in the context of a modern war. The Air Force had no opposition, and as a result learnt to take more risks than would have been possible under normal circumstances. On the whole an air of confidence prevailed. But the worst was to follow, for policing the ceasefire line tied down two-thirds of the Indian field force to holding the dominating heights in penny packets, an and this commitment continues till today.

Appendix

This defensive hibernation sapped the offensive spirit of the Indian Army as the years passed. The end of the little war brought up another phenomenon character assassination. Petty jealousies surfaced among the general officers and intrigues flourished, leading to the trial by court martial of Pritam Singh, the hero of Poonch, for alleged connivance in the theft of two carpets from the local palace. Although Pritam Singh was ostensibly on trial, the conspirators were bent on implicating Kalwant Singh and Mehar Singh.

It is said that Thimayya, a defence witness, stated "without Pritam there would have been no Poonch, and with Poonch would have gone these carpets. Why are you crucifying this good soldier for nothing?" Pritam Singh was unceremoniously dismissed from service. Kalwant Singh and Sant Singh were subsequently superseded by some of the generals involved in the plot who had not even heard a shot fired in anger. Baba Mehar Singh, by then a legendary figure in the services, resigned in disgust to become the personal pilot of a dethroned maharaja and this was to have serious repercussions later.

Meanwhile, General Carriappa replaced the British chief and the Indian Army settled down to peacetime soldiering. Kipper was a stickler for dress, spit and polish and soldierly deportment. He lived by rules and regulations and thrust this life on the Army to the extent that every officer was made to carry in his pocket the US Army cadets' prayer and his personal letter to all officers.

Appendix

He believed in stability and insisted that the sole criterion for promotion was seniority. It was a joke prevalent among officers those days that even if you were a donkey asleep underneath a blanket, when your turn came your ears would be pulled and you would be given an extra pip.

Carriappa submitted to the dictates of the then Defence Secretary H.M. Patel. He accepted a new pay code whereby an Indian commissioned officer's salary was reduced in relation to that of the civil services, while king's commissioned officers continued to draw the old rates of pay according to the British conditions of service, including overseas leave. Such disparities affected officers' morale to such an extent that some of our best talents like Colonel Leslie Sawhney left the Army for better prospects elsewhere. When questioned about the disparity of pay between KCIOs and ICOs, Carriappa replied: "After all, KCIOs are only a handful. Why do you grudge their privileges?" Good old Kipper belonged to the medieval period and refused to sense the winds of change.

"Sikh War with Pakistan!"

Excerpt taken from Narindar Singh Dhesi's book 'Sikh Soldier: At War'.

I have read in the recent past some Indian journalist calling 1965 the "Sikh War with Pakistan." I always wondered why this respected journalist called it a Sikh War and not India's War. If analyzed, this War was wholly fought by Sikh Generals.

Appendix

Almost all Senior Commanders in the Western Sector and the Punjab Sector were Sikhs. Lieutenant General Harbakhsh Singh, with his Chief of Staff, Major-General Joginder Singh, commanded the entire Western zone and was, as such, the principal architect of India's victory. Involved with planning at the Army headquarters was another Sikh General, Major-General Narinder Singh. Lieutenant General Joginder Singh Dhillon, a brilliant tactician, with Brigadier Parkash Singh Grewal, and Artillery Commander, Brigadier S.S. Kalha, commanded the troops operating in the Punjab and parts of Rajasthan. Major-General Niranjan Prasad was replaced mid-battle by Major-General Mohindar Singh as Division Commander in the Amritsar sector, the other Division Commander, in the Khem Karan sector, being Major-General Gurbaksh Singh. North of the Ravi, Major-General Rajinder Singh 'Sparrow', Commanding an Armoured Division in a lightning push into Pakistan, his Centurion tanks humbled Pakistan's prestigious American gifted Pattons and Chaffees. The Khem Karan sector, too, was turned into what came to be known as the graveyard of the Pakistani Patton tanks. South of the Satluj, Brigadier Bant Singh, Commanding an independent Sikh Brigade Group, defended stoutly an extensive border covering the entire Ferozepore and Ganga Nagar districts. To the North in Kashmir Major Ranjit Singh Dayal, later Lieutenant General - led his troops up the impenetrable Haji Pir Pass and captured it, inflicting a devastating blow on the enemy control in the area.

Bibliography

Amarinder Singh (2010) *The Last Sunset,* Roli Books, New Delhi

A.L. Saigal (1977) *Birth of an Air Force,* Palit & Palit, New Delhi

Birdwood (Reprint) *The Sikh Regiment.* The Naval & Military Press, Uckfield.

Dhesi N.S. (2012) *Sikh Soldier, Warriors & Generals*, The Naval & Military Press, Uckfield.

Dhesi N.S. (2014) *Sikh Soldier, At War,* The Naval & Military Press, Uckfield.

Gautam Sharma (1996) *Nationalisation of the Indian Army*, Allied Publishers, New Delhi.

Gurdip Singh Kler (1995) *Unsung Battles of 1962*, Lancer Publishers, New Delhi.

K.C. Praval (1955) *Indian Army, After Independence*, Lancer Publishers, New Delhi.

Khuswant Singh (1966) *History of the Sikhs*, Oxford University Press, Oxford.

Major Rifat Nadeem Ahmad, Major General Rafiuddin Ahmad (2006) *Unfaded Glory, The 8TH Punjab Regiment,* Naval & Military Press, Uckfield.

Merewether & Smith, (1919) *The Indian Corps in France,* John Murray, London.

Peter Bance (2004) *The Duleep Singhs*, Sutton publishing Ltd. Gloucestershire, UK.

Pradeep P. Barua (2003) *Gentlemen of the Raj*, Praeger Publishers, Westport, USA.

Bibliography

Pigot (Reprint) *14TH Punjab Regiment*, The Naval & Military Press, Uckfield.

Proudfoot (1991) *7TH Light Cavalry,* Lancer Publishers, New Delhi.

Raj Kumar, (2004) *Military System of the Sikhs*, Commonwealth Publishers, New Delhi.

Sagoo, Harbans (2001). *Banda Singh Bahadur and Sikh Sovereignty*. Deep & Deep Publications.

Sita Ram Kohli (1933) *Maharaja Ranjit Singh,* Guru Nanak Dev University, Amritsar.

Index

Afghans	12
Ajaib Singh, Captain	80
AJS Sandhu, Major General	6
Ajvir Singh Sandhu, Flying Officer	220
Aksai Chin	17
Akual Singh, Captain	117
Akyab Island	97
Aldershot	67
Amarjit Singh, Pilot Officer	147
Amba Alagi	49
Amreek Singh, Lieutenant Colonel	119
Amritsar	186
Anglo-Sikh Wars	20
Anup Singh Kalha, Brigadier	133
Arakan	149
Arjan Singh, Marshal of the Indian Air Force	158
Atma Singh, Major General	75
Aurangabad	64
Bakshish Singh Chimni, Major General	32
Baldev Singh Johl, Colonel	107
Baljit Singh, Brigadier General	111
Baluchistan	24
Balwant Singh, Lieutenant	86
Balwant Singh Lamba, Captain	29
Banda Bahadur	10
Bangkok	46
Basra	67
Battle of Imphal	69
Battle of Meiktilla	55
Benjit Singh Dhesi, Captain	216

Index

Bhajan Singh, Lieutenant Colonel	114
Bhupinder Singh, Pilot Officer	147
Bikram Chowk	99
Bikram Singh, Lieutenant General	94
Bir Hacheim	133
Blo Norton	22
Borneo	89
Brijinder Singh Nijjar, Lieutenant	218
Burma	41
Cambridge	20
Canada	146
Chillianwala	13
Chinese	17
Cranwell	144
Cyprus	129
Dal Khalsa	10
Daljinder Singh Virdee, Lieutenant	219
Daljit Singh, Major	112
Daljit Singh, Pilot Officer	147
Dartmouth	197
Daulatabad Fort	64
Daya Singh Bedi, Colonel	23
Dehradun	202
Dhaliwal BS, Lieutenant General	6,8
Digamber Singh Brar, Major General	61
Dr. Anthony Morton	6
Dulip Singh, Lieutenant Colonel	113
Egypt	26
Eleveden Hall	20

Index

Eritrea	22
Faqir of Ipi	67
France and Flanders	14
G. S. Chana, Lieutenant Colonel	162
Gallabat	95
General Biji Kaul	98
Gothic Line	62
Gujarat	13
Gulab Singh Dogra	12
Gurbachan Singh, Brigadier	25
Gurdial Singh, Colonel	70
Gurdip Singh Dhillon, Major General	29
A.S. Sandhu, Flight Lieutenant	221
Guru Gobind Singh	9
Harbhajan Singh, Lieutenant Commander	210
Hardev Singh, Lieutenant Commander	202
Hari Singh Nalwa, General	35
Harjinder Nagar	166
Harjinder Singh, Air Vice Marshal	164
Harmeet Singh Nijjar, Lieutenant	118
Guru Nanak	9
Habbaniya	149
Harjit Singh Randhawa, Major	119
Harjot Singh Gill, Captain	214
Harkirat Singh, Major General	129
Harmeet Singh Nijjar, Lieutenant	218
Hukma Singh Chimni, General	35
Hyderabad State forces	17
India	218
Indian Army	14

Index

Iran.	94
Iraq	94
Italians	76
Jammu	78
Japanese	82
Jagjeet Singh, Major	120
Jhangar	42
Jugjit Singh, Major	118
Kalwant Singh, Lieutenant General	40
Kampar	104
Kashmir	134
Kassala	95
Kenya	161
Khaisora	86
Khartoum	95
Kohat	77
Kota Bharu	86
Kulwant Singh Sandhu, Brigadier	90
Ladakh	98
Lady Ann Blanche Alice	20
Lakhbir Singh Gill, Major	108
Lakhinder Singh, Major General	48
Lal Singh	123
Laos	56
Lashkar	30
Laurie Michael Singh Dhesi	3
Libya	95

Index

Lysander	137
Mahabir Singh Dhillon, Major	100
Maharaja of Kashmir	137
Maharajah Dalip Singh	13
Maharajah Ranjit Singh	13
Makhand Singh, Captain	213
Malaya	26
Malaysia	107
Man Mohan Singh, Flying Officer	167
Minister Jawaharlal Nehru	43
Mirpur	42
Mohindar Singh Chopra, Major General	66
Mohinder Jit Singh, Lieutenant Colonel	113
Mohinder Singh Pujji, Squadron Leader	171
Mohmad	29
MS Ratra, Commodore	208
Mughals	121
Narain Singh, Captain	94
Naranjan Singh Gill, Colonel	45
Nawab Kapur Singh	10
Neel Singh, Lieutenant	219
Neil Singh Khepar, Captain	216
Nizam	16
North Africa	95
Pakistan	15
Palestine.	68
Panama	47
Pathans	11
Patiala State	168
Poonch	42

Index

Prem Singh Gyani, Lieutenant General	128
Prince Frederick Duleep Singh	21
Prince Victor Duleep Singh	20
Pritam Singh Chodhury, Major General	80
Prithipal Singh, Squadron Leader	155
Queen Victoria	20
Rajindar Singh, Major	55
Rajinder Singh Kalha, Colonel	91
Ramree Island	97
Rangoon	158
Saigon	56
Sandhurst	2
Sant Singh, Lieutenant General	35
Sarbjit Singh Kalha, Colonel	93
Sartaj Singh Gogna, Major	214
Sardar Hardit Singh Malik	144
Sarjit Singh Sindhu, Major	117
Sarjit Singh, Lieutenant Colonel	116
Satwari Cantonment	79
Shivdev Singh, Air Marshal	170
Sikh Kingdom	20
Sir Sunder Singh Majithia	45
Sukhdev Singh Gill, Colonel	115
Sukhdev Singh Cheema, Lieutenant	218
Syed Ata Hasnain, Lieutenant General	60
Tara Singh Bal, Major General	53
Tarlochan Singh Marwaha, Colonel	212
Tej Singh	12
Vir Singh, Major	72

Indian Navy

The author was not able to find the bio-data about the following naval officers that trained at Dartmouth:

Commander Kulwant Singh,	Commissioned in 1943
Rear Admiral A.P. Singh Bindra,	Commissioned in 1943
Daljit Singh Paintal,	Commissioned in 1945
Commodore JS Bawa,	Commissioned in 1946
Commodore I.S. Pantle	Commissioned in 1948
Commander R.S. Grewal	Commissioned in 1951
Commander Harbhajan Singh	Commissioned in 1951

ABOUT THIS BOOK

This is the story of the Sikh cadets that were trained at Sandhurst, Woolwich, Cranwell and Dartmouth in the United Kingdom. They played a crucial role in the defence of their respective countries with unflinching sense of duty, discipline and traditions of valour.

Narindar Singh Dhesi was born in 1940 at Eldoret in Kenya, where his father had migrated from the Punjab. He moved to England in 1957 and joined the British Army. After leaving the armed forces in 1964, he worked in the building and construction industry. He is married with four children and living in retirement at Southend on Sea, Essex, England.

He is the author of six books on Sikh Soldier i.e. ***Sikh Soldier: Battle Honours (ISBN 978184574891), Sikh Soldier: Gallantry Awards (ISBN 9781845749057), Sikh Soldier: Policing the Empire (ISBN 9781781519851), Sikh Soldier: Warriors and Generals (ISBN 978783310234,) Sikh Soldier: At War (ISBN 8781783311262), and Sikh Soldier: Forgotten Regiments (ISBN 7817833123351).***

They are available from the Naval and Military Press.

Email: narindardhesi@yahoo.co.uk

www.ingramcontent.com/pod-product-compliance
Lightning Source LLC
Chambersburg PA
CBHW071001160426
43193CB00012B/1872